Rise of the Data Lakehouse

Building the Data Lakehouse 2nd Edition

Bill Inmon

Ranjeet Srivastava

Technics Publications

115 Linda Vista, Sedona, Arizona, USA
https://www.TechnicsPub.com

Edited by Jamie Hoberman
Cover design by Lorena Molinari

First Printing First Edition 2021
First Printing Second Edition 2023

Copyright © 2023 by Bill Inmon and Ranjeet Srivastava

ISBN, print ed.   9781634627986
ISBN, Kindle ed.   9781634627993
ISBN, ePub ed.   9781634628006
ISBN, PDF ed.   9781634628020

Library of Congress Control Number: 2023932092

Preface

Dear reader,

I am thrilled to introduce Rise of the Data Lakehouse, the revised and updated version of my book, *Building the Data Lakehouse*. The highlight of this book is a brand new chapter that delves into the implementation details of the Databricks Lakehouse Platform and its various workloads, including data engineering, data warehouses, data streaming, data science and machine learning.

Whether you are new to the world of data lakehouses or are already well-versed in their capabilities, this book is a must-read for anyone looking to get the most out of their data management strategy.

Thank you for considering *Rise of the Data Lakehouse* - Why lakehouses are the data architecture of the future. I hope it serves as a valuable resource as you navigate the exciting world of data, analytics and AI.

Sincerely,

Bill Inmon

Contents

Introduction

Once the world had simple applications. But in today's world, we have all sorts of data, technology, hardware, and other gadgets. Data comes to us from a myriad of places and comes in many forms. And the volume of data is just crushing.

There are three different types of data that an organization uses for analytical purposes. First, there is classical structured data that principally comes from executing transactions. This structured data has been around the longest. Second, there is textual data from emails, call center conversations, contracts, medical records, and elsewhere. Once text was a "black box" that could only be stored but not analyzed by the computer.

Now, textual Extract, Transform, and Load (ETL) technology has opened the door of text to standard analytical techniques. Third, there is the world of analog/IoT. Machines of every kind, such as drones, electric eyes, temperature gauges, and wristwatches—all can generate data. Analog/IoT data is in a much rougher form than structured or textual data. And there is a tremendous amount of this data generated in an automated manner. Analog/IoT data is the domain of the data scientist.

At first, we threw all of this data into a pit called the "data lake." But we soon discovered that merely throwing data into a pit was a pointless exercise. To be useful—to be analyzed—data needed to (1) be related to each other and (2) have its analytical infrastructure carefully arranged and made available to the end user.

Unless we meet these two conditions, the data lake turns into a swamp, and swamps start to smell after a while.

A data lake that does not meet the criteria for analysis is a waste of time and money.

Enter the data lakehouse. The data lakehouse indeed adds the elements to the data lake to become useful and productive. Stated differently, if all you build is a data lake without turning it into a data lakehouse, you have just created an expensive eyesore. Over time that eyesore is going to turn into an expensive liability.

The first of those elements needed for analysis and machine learning is the analytical infrastructure. The analytical infrastructure contains a combination of familiar things and some things that may not be familiar. For example, the analytical infrastructure of the data lakehouse contains:

- Metadata
- Lineage of the data

- Volumetric measurements
- Historical records of creation
- Transformation descriptions

The second essential element of the data lakehouse needed for analysis and machine learning is recognizing and using the universal common connector. The universal common connector allows data of all varieties to be combined and compared. Without the universal common connector, it is very difficult (if not impossible) for the diverse types of data found in the data lakehouse to be related. But with the universal common connector, it is possible to relate any kind of data.

With the data lakehouse, it is possible to achieve a level of analytics and machine learning that is not feasible or possible any other way. But like all architectural structures, the data lakehouse requires an understanding of architecture and an ability to plan and create a blueprint.

CHAPTER 1

Evolution to the Data Lakehouse

Most evolutions occur over eons of time. The evolution occurs so slowly that the steps in the evolution are not observable on a day-to-day basis. Watching the daily progression of an evolution makes watching paint dry look like a spectator sport. However, the evolution of computer technology has progressed at warp speed, starting in the 1960s.

The evolution of technology

Once upon a time, life was simple when it came to the computer. Data went in, was processed, and data came out. In the beginning, there was paper tape. Paper tape was automated but stored a minuscule amount of data in a fixed format. Then came punched cards. One of the problems with punched cards was that they were in a fixed format. Huge volumes of punched cards consumed huge amounts of paper and dropping a deck of cards led to a tedious effort to get the cards back in order.

Then modern data processing began with magnetic tape, which opened up the door to the storage and usage of larger volumes of data not in a fixed format. The problem with magnetic tape was that you had to search the entire file to find a particular record. Stated differently, with magnetic tape files, you had to search data sequentially. And magnetic tapes were notoriously fragile, so storing data for long periods was not advisable.

Then came disk storage. Disk storage truly opened the door even wider to modern IT processing by introducing direct data access. With disk storage, you could go to a record directly, not sequentially. Although there were cost and availability issues early on, disk storage became much less expensive, and large volumes of disk storage became widely available over time.

Online transaction processing (OLTP)

The fact that data could be accessed directly opened up the door to high-performance, direct access applications.

With high-performance and direct data access, Online Transaction Systems (OLTP) became possible. Once online transaction processing systems became available, businesses found that computers had entered into the very fabric of the business. Now there could be online reservation systems, banking teller systems, ATM systems, and the like. Now computers could directly interact with customers.

In the early days of the computer, the computer was useful for doing repetitive activities. But with online transaction processing systems, the computer was useful for direct interaction with the customer. In doing so, the business value of the computer increased dramatically.

Computer applications

Very quickly, applications grew like weeds in the springtime. Soon there were applications everywhere.

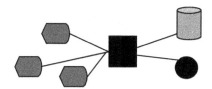

Figure 1-1. Lots of applications for lots of reasons.

The problem of data integrity

And with the growth of applications came a new and unanticipated problem. In the early days of the computer, the end user complained about not having his/her data. But after being inundated with applications, the end user then complained about not finding the *RIGHT* data.

The end user switched from not being able to find data to not being able to find the right data. This sounds like an almost trivial shift, but it was anything but trivial.

With the proliferation of applications came the problem of data integrity. The same data appeared in many places with sometimes different values. To make a decision, the end user had to find *which* version of the data was the right one to use among the many available applications. Poor business choices resulted when the end user did not find and use the right version of data.

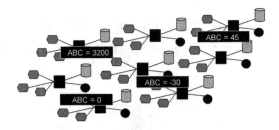

Figure 1-2. Trying to find the correct data on which to base decisions was an enormous task.

The challenge of finding the right data was a challenge that few people understood. But over time, people began to understand the complexity of finding the right data to use for decision making. People discovered that they needed a different architectural approach than simply building more applications. Adding more machines, technology, and consultants made matters relating to the integrity of data worse, not better.

Adding more technology exaggerated the problems of the lack
of integrity of data.

The data warehouse

Enter the data warehouse. The data warehouse led to disparate application data being copied into a separate physical location. Thus, the data warehouse became an architectural solution to an architectural problem.

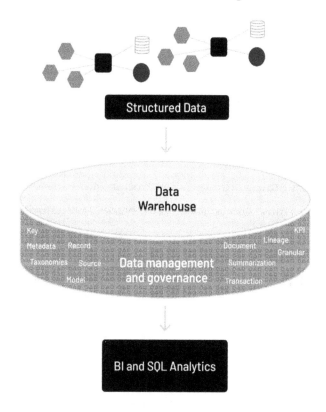

Figure 1-3. An entirely new infrastructure around the data warehouse was needed.

Merely integrating data and placing it into a physically separate location was only the start of the architecture. To be successful, the designer had to build an entirely new infrastructure around the data warehouse. The infrastructure that surrounded the data warehouse made the data found in the data warehouse usable and easily analyzed. Stated differently, as important as the data warehouse was, the end user found little value in the data warehouse without the surrounding analytical infrastructure. The analytical infrastructure included:

- **Metadata**—a guide to what data was located where
- **Data model**—an abstraction of the data found in the data warehouse
- **Data lineage**—the tale of the origins and transformations of data found in the data warehouse
- **Summarization**—a description of the algorithmic work to create the data in the data warehouse
- **KPIs**—where are key performance indicators found
- **ETL**—technology that allowed applications data to be transformed automatically into corporate data

The issue of historical data

Data warehousing opened other doors for analytical processing. Before data warehousing, there was no convenient place to store older and archival data easily and efficiently—it was normal for organizations to store a week, a month, or even a quarter's worth of data in their systems. But it was rare for an organization to store a year or five years' worth of data. But with data warehousing, organizations could store ten years or more.

And there was great value in being able to store a longer spectrum of time-valued data. For example, when organizations became interested in looking at a customer's buying habits, understanding past buying patterns led the way to understanding current and future buying patterns.

The past became a great predictor of the future.

Data warehousing then added the dimension of a greater length of time for data storage to the world of analysis. Now historical data was no longer a burden.

As important and useful as data warehouses are, for the most part, data warehouses focus on structured, transaction-based data. It is worth pointing out that many other data types are not available in the structured environment or the data warehouse.

The evolution of technology did not stop with the advent of structured data. Soon data appeared from many different and diverse sources. There were call centers. There was the internet. There were machines that produced data. Data seemed to come from everywhere. The evolution continued well beyond structured, transaction-based data.

The limitations of data warehouses became evident with the increasing variety of data (text, IoT, images, audio, videos, drones, etc.) in the enterprise. In addition, the rise of Machine Learning (ML) and Artificial Intelligence (AI) introduced iterative algorithms that required direct data access to data not based on SQL.

All the data in the organization

As important and useful as data warehouses are, for the most part, data warehouses are centered around structured data. But now, there are many other data types in the organization. To see what data resides in an organization, consider a simple graph.

Figure 1-4. A simple graph.

Structured data is typically transaction-based data generated by an organization to conduct day-to-day business activities. For example, textual data is data generated by letters, emails, and conversations within the organization. Other unstructured data has other sources, such as IoT, image, video, and analog-based data.

Structured data

The first type of data to appear was structured data. For the most part, structured data was a by-product of transaction processing. A record was written when a transaction was executed. This could be a sale, payment, phone call, bank activity, or other transaction type. Each new record had a similar structure to the previous record.

To see this similarity of processing, consider the making of a deposit in a bank. A bank customer walks up to the teller window and makes a deposit. The next person comes to the window and also makes a deposit. Although the account numbers and deposit amounts are different, the structures of both records are the same.

We call this "structured data" because the same data structure is written and rewritten repeatedly.

Typically when you have structured data, you have many records—one for each transaction that has occurred. So naturally, there is a high degree of business value placed on structured data for no other reason than transactions are very near the business's heart.

Textual data

The primary reason raw text is not very useful is that raw text must also contain context to be understood. Therefore, it is not sufficient to merely read and analyze raw text.

To analyze text, we must understand both the text and the context of the text.

However, we need to consider other aspects of text. We must consider that text exists in a language, such as English, Spanish, German, etc. Also, some text is predictable, but other text is not predictable. Analyzing predictable text is very different than analyzing unpredictable text. Another obstacle to incisive analysis is that the same word can have multiple meanings. The word "record" can mean a vinyl recording of a song. Or it can mean the speed of a race. Or other things. And other obstacles await the person that tries to read and analyze raw text.

Textual ETL

Fortunately, creating text in a structured format is a real possibility. There is technology known as textual ETL. With textual ETL, you can read the raw text and transform it into a standard database format, identifying both text and context. And in doing so, you can now start to blend structured data and text. Or you can do an independent analysis of the text by itself.

Analog data/IoT data

The operation of a machine, such as a car, watch, or manufacturing machine, creates analog data. As long as the machine is operating, it spews out measurements. The measurements may be of many things—temperature, chemical makeup, speed, time of day, etc. In fact, the analog data may be of many different variables measured and captured simultaneously.

Electronic eyes, temperature monitors, video equipment, telemetry, timers—there are many sources of analog data.

It is normal for there to be many occurrences of analog data. Depending on the machine and what processing is occurring, it is normal to take measurements every second, every ten seconds, or perhaps every minute.

In truth, most of the measurements—those within the band of normality—may not be very interesting or useful. But occasionally, there will be a measurement outside the band of normality that indeed is very interesting.

The challenge in capturing and managing analog and IoT data is in determining:

- What types of data to capture and measure
- The frequency of data capture
- The band of normality

Other challenges include the volume of data collected, the need to occasionally transform the data, finding and removing outliers, relating the analog data to other data, and so forth. As a rule, store data inside the band of normality in bulk storage and data outside the band of normality in a separate store.

Another way to store data is by relevancy to problem-solving. Traditionally, certain types of data are more relevant to solving a problem than other sorts of data.

There typically are three things that catch the attention of the person analyzing analog data:

- Specific values of data
- Trends of data across many occurrences
- Correlative patterns

Other types of unstructured data

The majority of the data generated by enterprises today falls under unstructured data—images, audio, and video content.

You cannot store this data in a typical database table as it normally lacks a tabular structure. Given the massive volume of analog and IoT data, storing and managing these datasets is very expensive.

It isn't easy to analyze unstructured data with SQL-only interfaces. However, with the advent of cheap blob storage in the cloud, elastic cloud compute and machine learning algorithms can access unstructured data directly— enterprises are beginning to understand the potential of these datasets.

Here are some emerging use cases for unstructured data.

Image Data
- Medical image analysis to help radiologists with X-Rays, CT, and MRI scans
- Image classification for hotels and restaurants to classify pictures of their properties and food
- Visual search for product discovery to improve the experience for e-commerce companies
- Brand identification in social media images to identify demographics for marketing campaigns

Audio Data
- Automated transcription of call-center audio data to help provide better customer service

- Conversational AI techniques to recognize speech and communicate in a similar way to human conversation
- Audio AI to map out the various acoustic signatures of machines in a manufacturing plant to proactively monitor the equipment

Video Data

- In-store analytic video analytics to provide people counting, queue analysis, heat maps, etc., to understand how people are interacting with products
- Video analytics to automatically track inventory and also detect product faults in the manufacturing process
- Video data to provide deep usage data, helping policy makers and governments decide when public infrastructure requires maintenance work
- Facial recognition to allow healthcare workers to be alerted if and when a patient with dementia leaves the facility and respond appropriately

Where is business value?

There are different kinds of business value associated with different classifications of data. First, there is business value for the day-to-day activities. Second, there is long-term strategic business value. Third, there is business value in the management and operation of mechanical devices.

Not surprisingly, there is a very strong relationship between structured data and business value. The world of transactions and structured data is where the organization conducts its day-to-day business. And there is also a strong relationship between textual data and business value. Text is the very fabric of the business.

But there is a different kind of business relationship between analog/IoT and today's business. Organizations are only beginning to understand the potential of analog/IoT data today with access to massive cloud computing resources and machine learning frameworks. For example, organizations use image data to identify quality defects in manufacturing, audio data in call centers to analyze customer sentiment, and video data of remote operations such as oil and gas pipelines to perform predictive maintenance.

The data lake

The data lake is an amalgamation of all of the different kinds of data found in the organization.

The first type of data in the lake is structured data. The second type of data is textual data. And the third type of data is analog/IoT data. There are many challenges with the data that resides in the data lake. But one of the biggest challenges is that the form and structure of analog/IoT data is very different from the classical structured data in the data warehouse. To complicate matters, the volumes of data across the different types of data found in the data lake are very different. As a rule, there is a very large amount of data found in the analog/IoT portion of the data lake compared to the volume of data found in other types of data.

The data lake is where enterprises offload all their data, given its low-cost storage systems with a file API that holds data in generic and open file formats, such as Apache Parquet and ORC. The use of open formats also made data lake data directly accessible to a wide range of other analytics engines, such as machine learning systems.

In the beginning, it was thought that all that was required was to extract data and place it in the data lake. Once in the data lake, the end user could just dive in and find data and do analysis. However, organizations quickly discovered that using the data in the data lake was a completely different story than merely having the data placed in the lake. Stated differently, the end user's needs were very different from the needs of the data scientist.

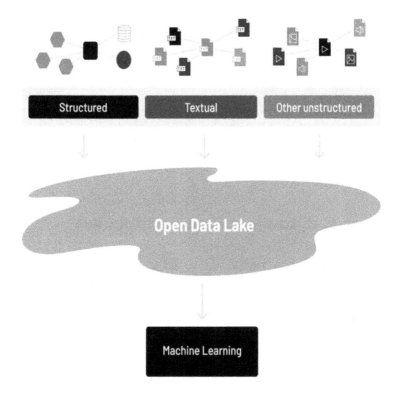

Figure 1-5. The data lake uses open formats.

The end user ran into all sorts of obstacles:

- Where was the data that was needed?
- How did one unit of data relate to another unit of data?
- Was the data up to date?
- How accurate was the data?

Many of the promises of the data lakes have not been realized due to the lack of some critical infrastructure features: no support for transactions, no enforcement of data quality or governance, and poor performance optimizations. As a result, most of the data lakes in the enterprise have become data swamps.

In a data swamp, data just sits there are no one uses it. In the data swamp, data just rots over time.

Current data architecture challenges

A common analytical approach is to use multiple systems—a data lake, several data warehouses, and other specialized systems, resulting in three common problems:

1. **Expensive data movement with dual architecture**. More than 90% of analog/IoT data is stored in data lakes due to its flexibility from open direct access to files and low cost, as it uses cheap storage. To overcome the data lake's lack of performance and quality issues, enterprises use ETL (Extract/Transform/Load) to copy a small subset of data in the data lake to a downstream data warehouse for the most important decision support and BI applications. This dual system architecture requires continuous engineering to ETL data between the lake and warehouse. Each ETL step risks incurring failures or introducing bugs that reduce data quality—keeping the data lake and

warehouse consistent is difficult and costly. At the same time, ETL can integrate the data.

2. **Limited support for machine learning**. Despite much research on the confluence of ML and data management, none of the leading machine learning systems, such as TensorFlow, PyTorch, and XGBoost, work well on top of warehouses. Unlike Business Intelligence (BI) which extracts a small amount of data, ML systems process large datasets using complex non-SQL code.

3. **Lack of openness**. Data warehouses lock data into proprietary formats that increase the cost of migrating data or workloads to other systems. Given that data warehouses primarily provide SQL-only access, it is hard to run any other analytics engines, such as machine learning systems against the data warehouses.

Emergence of the data lakehouse

From the data swamp, there emerges a new class of data architecture called the *data lakehouse*. The data lakehouse has several components:

- Data from the structured environment
- Data from the textual environment

- Data from the analog/IoT environment
- An analytical infrastructure allowing data in the lakehouse to be read and understood

A new open and standardized system design enables analog/IoT data analysis by implementing similar data structures and data management features to those found in a data warehouse but operating directly on the kind of low-cost storage used for data lakes.

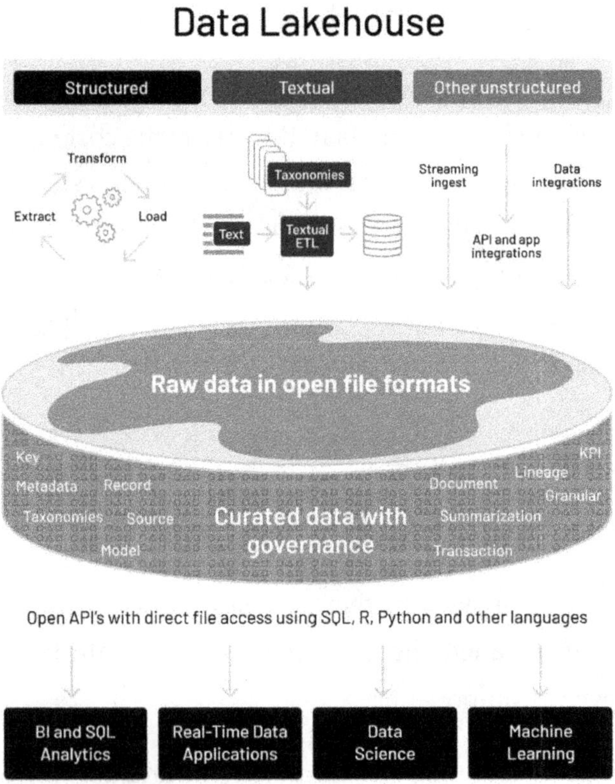

Data Lakehouse

| Structured | Textual | Other unstructured |

Transform

Extract — Load

Taxonomies

Text → Textual ETL

Streaming ingest

Data integrations

API and app integrations

Raw data in open file formats

Key

Metadata   Record

Taxonomies   Source

Model

Curated data with governance

Document

Summarization

Transaction

KPI

Lineage

Granular

Open API's with direct file access using SQL, R, Python and other languages

| BI and SQL Analytics | Real-Time Data Applications | Data Science | Machine Learning |

Figure 1-6. The data lakehouse architecture.

The data lakehouse architecture addresses the key challenges of current data architectures discussed in the previous section by building on top of existing data lakes.

Here are the six steps to build out the analog/IoT component of the data lakehouse architecture:

1. Taking a lake-first approach

Leverage the analog and IoT data already found in the data lake, as the data lake already stores most structured, textual, and other unstructured data on low-cost storage such as Amazon S3, Azure Blob Storage, or Google Cloud.

2. Bringing reliability and quality to the data lake

- Transaction support leverages ACID transactions to ensure consistency as multiple parties concurrently read or write data, typically using SQL
- Schema support provides support for DW schema architectures like star/snowflake-schemas and provides robust governance and auditing mechanisms
- Schema enforcement provides the ability to specify the desired schema and enforce it, preventing bad data from causing data corruption
- Schema evolution allows data to change constantly, enabling the end user to make changes to a table

schema that can be applied automatically, without the need for cumbersome DDL

3. Adding governance and security controls

- DML support through Scala, Java, Python, and SQL APIs to merge, update and delete datasets, enabling compliance with GDPR and CCPA and also simplifying use cases like change data capture
- History provides records details about every change made to data, providing a full audit trail of the changes
- Data snapshots enable developers to access and revert to earlier versions of data for audits, rollbacks, or to reproduce experiments
- Role-based access control provides fine-grained security and governance for row/columnar level for tables

4. Optimizing performance

Enable various optimization techniques, such as caching, multi-dimensional clustering, z-ordering, and data skipping, by leveraging file statistics and data compaction to right-size the files.

5. Supporting machine learning

- Support for diverse data types to store, refine, analyze and access data for many new applications, including images, video, audio, semi-structured data, and text

- Efficient non-SQL direct reads of large volumes of data for running machine learning experiments using R and Python libraries
- Support for DataFrame API via a built-in declarative DataFrame API with query optimizations for data access in ML workloads, since ML systems such as TensorFlow, PyTorch, and XGBoost have adopted DataFrames as the main abstraction for manipulating data
- Data versioning for ML experiments, providing snapshots of data enabling data science and machine learning teams to access and revert to earlier versions of data for audits and rollbacks or to reproduce ML experiments

6. Providing openness

- Open file formats, such as Apache Parquet and ORC
- Open API provides an open API that can efficiently access the data directly without the need for proprietary engines and vendor lock-in
- Language support for not only SQL access but also a variety of other tools and engines, including machine learning and Python/R libraries

Comparing data warehouse and data lake with data lakehouse

	Data warehouse	Data lake	Data lakehouse
Data format	Closed, proprietary format	Open format	Open format
Types of data	Structured data, with limited support for semi-structured data	All types: Structured data, semi-structured data, textual data, unstructured (raw) data	All types: Structured data, semi-structured data, textual data, unstructured (raw) data
Data access	SQL-only	Open APIs for direct access to files with SQL, R, Python, and other languages	Open APIs for direct access to files with SQL, R, Python, and other languages
Reliability	High quality, reliable data with ACID transactions	Low quality, data swamp	High quality, reliable data with ACID transactions
Governance and security	Fine-grained security and governance for row/columnar level for tables	Poor governance as security needs to be applied to files	Fine-grained security and governance for row/columnar level for tables

	Data warehouse	Data lake	Data lakehouse
Performance	High	Low	High
Scalability	Scaling becomes exponentially more expensive	Scales to hold any amount of data at low cost, regardless of type	Scales to hold any amount of data at low cost, regardless of type
Use case support	Limited to BI, SQL applications, and decision support	Limited to machine learning	One data architecture for BI, SQL, and machine learning

The data lakehouse architecture presents an opportunity comparable to the one seen during the early years of the data warehouse market. The unique ability of the lakehouse to manage data in an open environment, blend all varieties of data from all parts of the enterprise, and combine the data science focus of the data lake with the end user analytics of the data warehouse will unlock incredible value for organizations.

CHAPTER 2

Data Scientists and End Users

First applications, then data warehouses, and then came a whole host of types of data. The volume of data and the diversity of data were bewildering. Soon these data types were placed in a data lake.

The data lake

Figure 2-1. The first rendition of a data lake was a repository of raw data. Data was simply placed into the data lake for anyone to analyze or use. The data lake data came from a wide variety of sources.

The analytical infrastructure

As time passed, we discovered the need for another data lake component: the analytical infrastructure. The analytical infrastructure was built from the raw data found in the data lake, and did many functions such as:

- Identify how data related to each other
- Identify the timeliness of data
- Examine the quality of the data
- Identify the lineage of data

Figure 2-2. The analytical infrastructure consisted of many different components, which we will describe in a later chapter.

Different audiences

The analytical infrastructure served one audience and the data lake served a different audience.

The primary audience served by the data lake was the data scientist.

Figure 2-3. The data scientist used the data lake to find new and interesting patterns and data trends in the organization.

The end user was the other type of community served by the data lake and the analytical infrastructure.

Figure 2.4. The end user's role was to keep the business moving forward productively and profitably on an ongoing basis.

The tools of analysis

One distinct difference between the end user and data scientist was the tools used to analyze data. The data scientist uses primarily statistical analytical tools.

Occasionally, the data scientist uses exploratory tools, but the data scientist uses statistical analysis tools for the most part.

The end user addresses data analysis in a completely different manner. The end user uses tools of simple calculation and visualization. The end user looks to create charts, diagrams, and other visual representations of data.

The data scientist tools operate on rough accumulations of data. The end user tools operate on uniform, well-defined data.

Visualization   Statistics

Figure 2.5. There is a very basic difference in the data that the two different communities operate on.

What is being analyzed?

Another difference between the data scientist and end user is that the two roles look for different things. The data science community is looking for new and profound patterns and trends in the data. In doing so, once discovering the patterns and trends, the data scientist can improve the life and profitability of the organization.

The end user is not interested in discovering new patterns of data. Instead, the end user is interested in recalculating and reexamining old patterns of data. For example, the end user is interested in monthly and quarterly KPIs covering profitability, new customers, new types of sales, etc.

KPIs
Quarterly profits

The mind of a 6 year old
The impact of a new competitive product

Figure 2.6. The data that the data scientist is interested in is very different from the end user's.

The analytical approaches

The analytical approaches taken by the data scientist and the end user are very different as well.

The data scientist uses a heuristic model of analysis. In the heuristic approach, the next step of analysis depends on the results obtained from the previous steps. When the data scientist first starts an analysis, the data scientist does not know what will be discovered or if anything will be discovered. In many cases, the data scientist discovers nothing. In other cases, the data scientist uncovers useful patterns that have never before been seen or recognized.

The end user operates entirely differently from the data scientist. The end user operates on the basis of regularly occurring patterns of data. The end user relies upon simple methods of calculation.

Calculation
Regular usage

Discovery
Irregular usage

Figure 2.7. The end user repeats the same analysis over and over on different segments of time. The data scientist operates in a mode of discovery.

Types of data

The data scientist operates on data with a low level of granularity that is widely diverse. Typically the data scientist works with data generated by a machine. Part of the exploration experience is the ability to roam over and examine a wide variety of different kinds of data.

The end user operates on summarized (or lightly summarized) data that is highly organized and appears regularly. Each month, each week, each day, the same type of data is examined and recalculated.

Summarization
Highly organized data

Low granularity
Wide diversity of data

Figure 2.8. Even the types of data the different communities operate on are different.

Given the stark differences in the needs of the different communities, it is no surprise that the different communities are attracted to different parts of the data lake.

Does this difference in attraction preclude the different communities from looking at data that is foreign to them?

The answer is not at all. There is no reason why the end user cannot look at and use the raw data found in the data lake. And conversely, there is no reason why the data scientist cannot use the analytical infrastructure.

Figure 2.9. The data scientist is attracted to the raw data found in the data lake, and the end user is attracted to the data found in the analytical infrastructure.

Indeed, the data scientist may well find the analytical infrastructure to be useful. However, although data scientists learn techniques for data analysis, when they go into the real world, they become data garbage men, as they spend 95% of their time cleaning data and 5% of their time doing data analysis.

There are then very different types of people that use the data lakehouse for very different purposes. The purpose of the data lakehouse is to serve all the different communities.

CHAPTER 3

Different Types of Data in the Data Lakehouse

The data lakehouse is an amalgamation of different types of data. Each of the different types of data has their own physical characteristics.

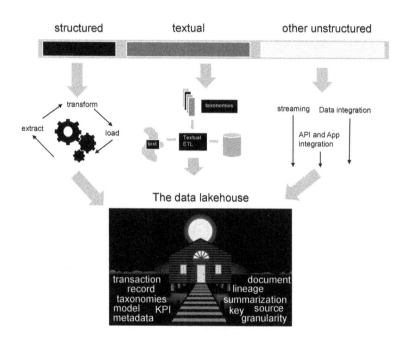

Figure 3-1. A data lakehouse and its infrastructure.

The data lakehouse consists of:

- A data lake, where raw amounts of text are placed
- An analytical infrastructure, where descriptive information is made available to the end user
- A collection of different kinds of data—structured, textual, and other unstructured data

The data found in the data lakehouse is open.

Let's dive deeper into each of these components.

Types of data

The three different types of data found in the data lakehouse include:

- Structured data—transaction-based data
- Textual data—data from conversations and written text
- Other unstructured data—analog data and IoT data, typically machine-generated data

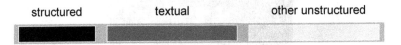

Figure 3-2. The three different types of data found in the data lakehouse.

Structured data

The earliest type of data to appear in computers was structured data. For the most part, structured data comes from the execution of transactions. A transaction executes and one or more structured records are written from the data that flows from the transaction.

The structured environment contains records. There is a uniform structure of the record for each occurrence. The records contain different kinds of information—keys, attributes, and other kinds of information. In addition, some indexes help with finding the location of a given structured record.

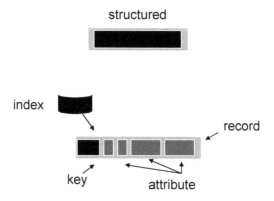

Figure 3-3. The physical elements of the structured environment.

The records are created in the structured environment via a database, where they can be accessed individually or collectively. Of course, records can be deleted or modified once entered into the database.

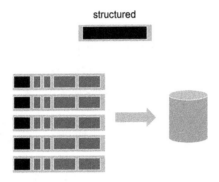

Figure 3-4. The inclusion of structured records in a database.

Textual data

The second type of data found in the data lakehouse is textual data. Textual data can come from anywhere—telephone conversations, email, the Internet, and so forth. As a rule, it does not do any good to store raw text in the data lakehouse. Instead, it is normal to store text in a database format. By storing text in a database format, analytical tools can be used against the text. A data lakehouse is capable of storing raw text, if that is what the business needs.

There are—at a minimum—certain types of textual data that are necessary to store in the data lakehouse:

- The source of the data
- The word of interest
- The context of the word
- The byte address of the word within the document

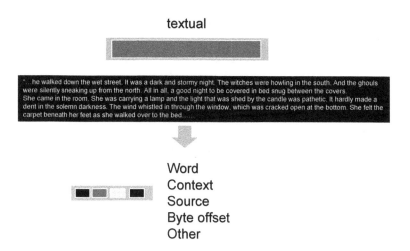

Figure 3-5. Types of textual data that are necessary to store in the data lakehouse.

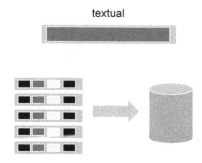

Figure 3-6. The resulting database after the text has been transformed into a database structure.

Other unstructured data

The third type of data found in the data lakehouse is the other unstructured category of data. This typically means analog data and IoT data, which are generated and collected by machines. There can be any number of types of measurements:

- Time of day
- Temperature
- Speed of processing
- Machine doing the processing
- Sequence number of processing

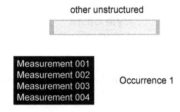

Figure 3-7. The types of measurement collected by the machine depend entirely on the type of data being captured and the machinery participating in the project.

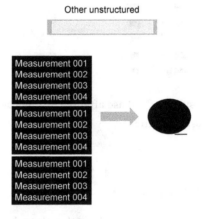

Figure 3-8. The measurements are captured in a periodic sequence— every second, every ten seconds, every minute, etc. Then the measurements are placed in a database.

Different volumes of data

When comparing the sheer volume of data in the different environments of the data lakehouse, there is a stark difference. The volume of data found in the structured environment is typically the smallest amount of data. The volume of data found in the textual environment is greater than in the structured environment. Still, less than the volume found in the other unstructured environment (the analog/IoT environment). And the volume of data found in the other unstructured environment is the greatest of all.

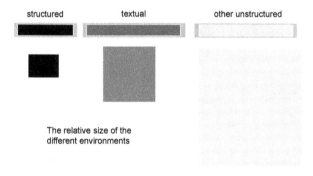

Figure 3-9. Volume comparisons will vary from company to company. But in general, this is the pattern.

Relating data across the diverse types of data

One of the more important features of the different physical environments found in the data lakehouse environment is relating the data from one environment to the next. When doing analytics on the data lakehouse, relating data from different environments is often a very useful thing to do.

It is necessary to have a common key in the environments to do analytics. There are different kinds of common keys that can be used, depending on the environment. However, some data defies the existence of a common key. In some cases, there simply is no common key.

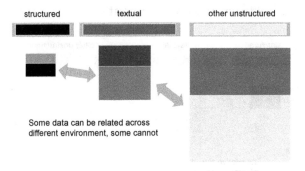

Figure 3-10. There is a need for a common key to do analytics and sometimes data simply does not have a common key.

Segmenting data based on probability of access

The analog and the IoT environment often place all of their data on bulk media. It is less expensive to do so, and it is expedient at the moment of storage of the data. But the problem with data placement in bulk storage is that bulk storage is not optimal for analysis. So, an alternate strategy is to place some of the analog and IoT data in bulk storage and the remainder in standard disk storage. The data placed in bulk storage has a low probability of access, and the data placed in disk storage has a high probability of access.

This arrangement of data accommodates the need for storage of large amounts of data balanced against the need for analytical processing of some of the data.

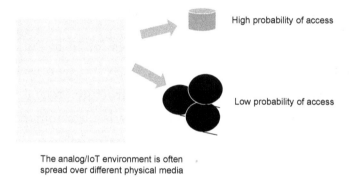

High probability of access

Low probability of access

The analog/IoT environment is often spread over different physical media

Figure 3-11. The segmented arrangement of data across different physical media.

Relating data in the IoT and the analog environment

The data found in the analog and the IoT environment may or may not be related.

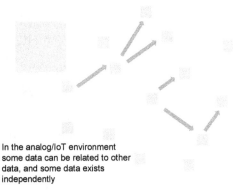

In the analog/IoT environment
some data can be related to other
data, and some data exists
independently

Figure 3-12. Some types of data in the analog and the IoT
environment can be easily and naturally related, while other data
found in the analog and the IoT environment is stand-alone data
that cannot be easily related to other data.

There is then a diversity of data types found in the data lakehouse. Each type of data has its own set of considerations regarding volume, structure, relatability, and other characteristics. When there is no common key across the different types of data, it is possible to use a universal connector.

A universal connector is a way to connect data when there is
no formal method.

There are a host of universal common connectors, such as:

- Geography/location
- Time
- Dollar amounts
- Name

As a simple example of the usage of a universal common connector, consider geography. Suppose that there is a large collection of X-rays. The X-rays are a study of bone density. The bone X-rays come from a variety of states.

The end user chooses two states—California and Maryland for analysis. All the X-rays from California are gathered together. Another collection is made of X-rays from Maryland. Finally, the end user makes an independent analysis of the X-rays from these two states.

Now, in the structured environment, the many purchases of medications that relate to bone density loss are selected. First, those medications from Maryland and California are selected. The end user determines the differences in the sale of different medications in each state. Then the X-rays are studied to determine what is the difference between bone densities in California and Maryland. The bone density analysis is now done against the states using the bone differential analysis in each state as measured against the consumption of medications in each state.

Note that there is no key structure that ties the bone X-rays to the purchase of medications. The only thing that ties the data together is the geography selected for the analysis and that bone density information is gathered.

The same sort of analysis can be done using dollar amounts, time, and so forth. There are, however, other universal common connectors. Such as for humans:

- Sex
- Age
- Race
- Weight
- Other body measurements

These universal connectors can be used for relating data across the different types of data.

The analytical infrastructure

Of course, the analytical infrastructure derives from the raw data found in the data lake. In many ways, the analytical infrastructure is like the card catalog in a large library. Consider what happens when you enter a large library. How do you find a book? Do you start to walk from stack to stack, sequentially searching for your book? If you take this approach, plan to be in the library for a long time. Instead, you quickly and efficiently search the card catalog. Once you have located your book in the card catalog, you know exactly where to go in the library to find your book. The analytical infrastructure plays the same role as the card catalog.

The analytical infrastructure provides a quick and easy reference to where the data you wish to analyze is found in the data lake.

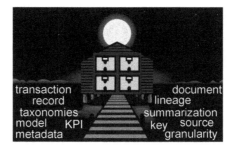

Figure 3-13. The analytical infrastructure plays the same role as the card catalog.

Once the data is found, it is then open for analysis and access. There are many ways to read and analyze the data found in the data lake and the analytical infrastructure:

- SQL, R, and Python
- BI tools, such as Tableau, Qlik, Excel, PowerBI
- Real-time applications
- Data science and statistical analysis
- Machine learning

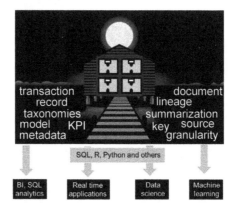

Figure 3-14. There are many ways to read and analyze the data found in the data lake and the analytical infrastructure.

CHAPTER 4

The Open Environment

The unstructured portion of the data lakehouse is built on open APIs and open file formats, like Apache Parquet and ORC, so the data can be written once in a single location and either processed in place or shared using open source software.

Open source includes code, community, and creativity.

Open source exists in an open public forum. Open source entails repositories for all to observe and interact. When an open source project solves a high-value problem, a community quickly rallies around it. The strength of the community comes from its diversity. Large projects will have contributors that span research institutions and industries from geographies around the world.

These projects draw upon the global talent pool of volunteers who are all motivated to improve the project and collectively benefit from the knowledge of experts who may work in completely separate domains. The pace of innovation in these projects cannot be matched by a single vendor alone. As the popularity of the projects grow, so too does the number of resources trained on how to leverage the technology, making it easier for companies to source talent into their organizations.

The evolution of open systems

The evolution of open big data systems began with the need for Internet-based companies to process ever-increasing amounts of data. It started with clickstream web log data. Then the smartphone revolution accelerated the need for distributed systems to process photos, audio, video, and geospatial data. This wide and diverse variety of data necessitated a different type of architecture which ultimately gave rise to the data lake. As the size of datasets increased, it was no longer feasible to copy data from one system to another for analysis. Instead, open source engines were built which could ingest, process, and write to these data lakes in parallel for maximum throughput.

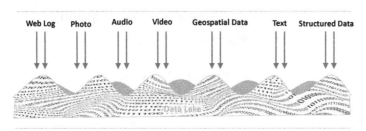

Figure 4-1. Variety of data ingestion into open source and open platform.

The data collected in these massive data lakes gave new digital upstarts a competitive edge. Amazon became famous for its recommendation engine based on the purchase history of its users. Whenever a user would pick a product to purchase, they would be prompted with a section showing other products purchased by customers who bought the same selected product. Today, customer preferences have evolved so that the picture of a selected item can be matched in real-time with similar items in inventory that share attributes of style. These advanced analytics use cases are all performed, at scale, using open source libraries on open programming languages such as Python and R. Researchers and practitioners who are experts in their field develop these libraries.

Moreover, these are libraries that students can use while training to be data scientists and data engineers. Most new graduates in the field of data science are learning their craft on non-proprietary software. Therefore, the enterprises that accommodate these open languages and libraries will be the most attractive for the next generation of data practitioners.

Innovation today

Open source software is one of the driving forces for innovation in the world of data. Data practitioners can use open source tools to construct an entire data stack from storage to the end-user tools and everything in between. Vendors who offer managed solutions around open source software reduce the risk and cost of hosting the software while retaining portability benefits. Given the forces of evolution at work, consider the different aspects of openness in the lakehouse architecture.

The unstructured portion of the lakehouse builds on open standard open file formats

The data lakehouse solves the lock-in challenges by building on top of open file formats that are supported by the vast majority of tools. Apache Parquet has become the de facto file format to store data for the unstructured portion of a data lakehouse. Parquet is an open binary file format that persists data in a columnar manner so that tabular data can be stored and retrieved efficiently.

When datasets need to be accessed, primarily for machine learning, the common pattern is to first export this data out of the data warehouse to distributed storage. Then data is ingested in parallel for model training and analysis. At a large scale, this constant exporting of data is impractical. Exporting terabytes or petabytes of data is expensive and can take hours or days. Ironically enough, the format that the data is typically exported to is Apache Parquet. Because a lakehouse writes the data once in this open format, it can be read many times without the need for exporting and duplicating.

The use and adoption of Parquet are so widespread that it can be easily shared across tools. Every distributed query engine and ETL tool supports it. If a better query engine is developed, companies can easily adopt it without exporting and transforming their data.

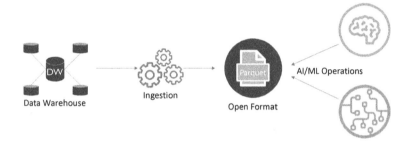

Figure 4-2. Cognitive and AI/ML operations from the data warehouse.

Open source lakehouse software

One of the key tenets of the unstructured portion of the lakehouse architecture is that it is open. This requires that the unstructured portion of the lakehouse adopt open file formats, open standards, open APIs, and be built upon open source software.

The open source community addresses the data swamp issue with the unstructured portion of the data lakes by creating open metadata layers to enable data management features such as ACID transactions, zero-copy cloning, and time travel to past versions of a table.

ACID is an acronym to certify that changes to data are Atomic, Isolated, Consistent, and Durable. A system with these properties prevents data from becoming corrupted. Zero-copy cloning is what enables a table to be copied instantaneously without duplicating the data. Time travel allows queries to be run against tables at a specific point in time. This can generate query results based on how a table was represented in the past.

These open metadata layers transform the unstructured portion of the data lake from being managed at the file-level to a logical table-level. Examples of this transformation include Delta Lake (created by Databricks), Hudi (created by Uber), and Iceberg (created by Netflix). These metadata layers are the combination of open APIs combined with open file formats. They represent an open logical data access layer that is implemented on top of the object storage services of all the major public cloud providers.

This foundational lakehouse logical layer is what separates a data lake from a data lakehouse. Data lakes were really well suited for machine learning applications but suffered from their lack of ACID transactions. The unstructured portion of the lakehouse logical layer is what enables fast queries during simultaneous ETL. It is equivalent to the transaction logs embedded inside databases but distributed and scalable. ACID transactions ensure that data is inserted, updated, merged, or deleted in the lakehouse without fear of data corruption or failure of simultaneous queries. This has enabled streaming ETL to keep the unstructured portion of the lakehouse fresh and provide real-time reporting.

Training machine learning models requires access to large amounts of data. If that data is in a data warehouse, the first step is typically to export the data into distributed storage in an open file format so that the model can be trained against it. It is important to reference the exact dataset used to train a model so that it can be reproduced in the future when it needs to be retrained. This duplicated export data will need to be retained to do so, or the data will need to be exported again each time the model is retrained.

By comparison, the unstructured portion of the lakehouse does not need to export datasets. The data is persisted once, and then multiple engines can be connected to the lakehouse to perform their processing. If a machine learning model needs to be trained, it can query the unstructured portion of the lakehouse directly without copying data. A lakehouse keeps history of the changes to the data and allows queries to be run "as of" a point in time. This enables an ML model to be reproduced using the exact dataset used to train it without duplicating any data. Because the unstructured portion of the lakehouse logical layer is open, it has quickly garnered the support of open source processing engines for SQL, ETL, streaming, and machine learning. Any engine that chooses to implement an open lakehouse logical layer will have access to consistent views of the data on all of the major public cloud storage systems and fast query performance. Furthermore, if a new engine offers characteristics that apply to needed use cases, they can be applied without a costly migration.

Lakehouse provides open APIs beyond SQL

SQL has long been the lingua franca of data analysis. This has been the only way to interact with data warehouses. However, each vendor offers its own proprietary API for stored procedures—typically for performing data transformation. For example, the stored procedures written for Teradata cannot be easily ported to Oracle or vice versa. The ability for organizations to move their workloads between different vendors' data systems is very time-consuming and very expensive. In recent years, a new class of dataframe APIs has emerged for working with data in languages such as Python and R. This has been the primary interface for data scientists. A dataframe is a class within a programing language with functions that are easy to chain together for manipulating data. More advanced analysis of video, images, and audio data is performed using deep learning libraries for machine learning. These APIs are open and capable of being leveraged at scale in a lakehouse alongside SQL for tabular data. These open APIs are enabling a fast-growing ecosystem of tools for ETL, ML, and visualization.

The unstructured portion of the lakehouse platform provides open APIs to access all types of data using SQL, Python, and other languages. These APIs are developed and improved by a community out in the open to garner fast and wide adoption if they address a critical problem. When an application implements an Open API, it becomes portable across environments and provides insurance for future migration, if needed. The unstructured portion of the data lakehouse ensures that a familiar SQL API can be used for tables, and data science-focused dataframe APIs in Python/R can be used for files.

Lakehouse enables open data sharing

Just as people share emails, they need to share data. Shared data includes granular data in large volumes, real-time data, and unstructured data such as pictures or videos. In addition, organizations need to share data with their customers, suppliers, and partners.

For too long, companies have been sharing data by encoding it into CSV files or complicated fixed-length formats and then transmitting it via File Transfer Protocol (FTP). FTP was an early point-to-point method of uploading and downloading files. It was left to the data consumer to translate the file format specification into ETL routines themselves. Some of these file specifications can run hundreds of pages long. Not only is this an inefficient use of engineer time, but of storage too. The exact same data is being duplicated many times over within the same public clouds.

Several cloud data warehouses offer data sharing functionality, but all are proprietary and force the solution through a single vendor. This creates friction between the data providers and the consumers, who inevitably run on different platforms. This can lead to data providers needing to duplicate their datasets, and in some cases, covering the cost for their consumers to access the data. It can also result in delays of up to months as consumers work to obtain the necessary internal approvals from IT, security, and procurement to deploy such technology.

An open approach to data sharing is required to break down these barriers. Open data formats, such as Apache Parquet, have already been adopted by open APIs and nearly all data tools. By sharing data in these open formats, existing tools can easily consume the data. Recipients do not need to use the same platform as the provider. Shared data via open file formats can be accessed directly by Business Intelligence (BI) tools or by open dataframe API for R and Python libraries. Distributed query engines can process large volumes of data without deploying any extra platform on the consumer side. Moreover, the data does not need to be copied. It can be written once by the provider and shared many times. The public cloud is a perfect place to store such data. The scalability and global availability of object storage enable consumers to access the data from any public cloud or even on-prem — regardless of the size of the dataset. The cloud already has the functionality to provide strict privacy and compliance requirements. Open data sharing in the cloud can be achieved without sacrificing security or the ability to audit access.

Lakehouse supports open data exploration

An open revolution has been taking place on data visualization. Historically, data was visualized via charts and graphs via proprietary business intelligence tools. With the advent of open visualization libraries, data could now be visualized in various ways across languages such as R, Python, and Javascript.

A new way to explore data came with the advent of notebook applications, which allows a user to create a series of "cells" in which code could be written and executed in real-time. The output could be visualized in tables or any of the aforementioned open visualization libraries. This new user interface has become popularized by the open source Jupyter project. The format by which Jupyter persists its notebooks has become a defacto standard that other notebook vendors adhere to when importing and exporting.

The notebook interface became popular at the same time as the field of data science was heating up. Data scientists were being employed not just to report on historical data, but also to use this data as a means of training statistical models, which could then be used to predict future outcomes. The most popular machine learning libraries are all open source.

When researchers in academia create and publish new machine learning algorithms, they do so using these open platforms. For example, there were 2,000 AI papers published at the 2020 NeurIPS conference (the top AI research conference). Many were published with code for the new algorithms they propose, and none of them run on data warehouses. All the ones with code can run on open machine learning libraries.

Lakehouse simplifies discovery with open data catalogs

Data catalogs and data discovery are two of the more developing areas of the open data ecosystem. Metadata has always been an important part of a data platform, but it hasn't always been elevated with tools to serve it up in a useful way to business users. Too often, different groups within an organization develop the same metrics but with slightly different meanings. The groups did not have any way of discovering that such metrics already existed, much less how to access them or easily understand how they were calculated. The result is redundant data being transformed and maintained by many groups.

Modern internet companies, such as LinkedIn, Netflix, and Lyft, have identified this in their own environments, created their own catalogs, and open sourced them. These catalogs can centralize the metadata for all of an enterprise's data assets. They can capture the lineage for how these data assets are sourced and transformed upstream and which systems consume the data downstream. These catalogs also embed powerful search and visualizations. This allows any user to search for metrics or datasets in the organization and identify the owner to request access. By having access to lineage and metadata around ETL job run times, these new catalogs can proactively alert owners that a target table may not get loaded soon enough to meet the expected time of arrival. This is detected based upon monitoring upstream jobs earlier in the process.

One of the reasons there is an explosion in open data catalogs is that they were created in companies largely using open source technology for their ETL, storage, and data exploration. Since the industry has coalesced around a few very popular open source projects for each domain, the question of "which systems do I integrate metadata with" becomes much easier to prioritize. These types of solutions have been developed before by proprietary software vendors. However, each vendor integrated well with their own tools and less so with competing vendors. Each vendor wants to get customers to use their entire stack. This impacts the ability to collect the full lineage or present it in a usable format to make decisions.

This new generation of open data catalogs is taking a different approach and is quickly gaining traction to help enterprises integrate their metadata and make it discoverable to the right people at the right time.

Lakehouse leverages cloud architecture

Migrating from an on-premise data warehouse to a different proprietary data warehouse in the cloud will not unlock portability or the innovation velocity that comes with an open data lakehouse. The public cloud has reshaped analytics by offering managed services of open source projects and by separating the compute from storage. One of the early concerns of open source software was the lack of enterprise readiness. If one were to download an open source project and run the software, that user assumes responsibility for that instance's maintainability, reliability, security, and scalability. Cloud managed services addressed this by hosting managed services of open source software with guarantees around security, compliance, and SLAs.

The public cloud completely disrupted the economics of data management by decoupling how compute and storage are priced. Prior to the public cloud, a data warehouse needed to have its capacity planned and paid for months in advance. The capacity had to allow for sufficient storage of data, indexes, and backups, along with a sufficient CPU and memory to handle the peak workloads for BI and ETL. These things were all tightly coupled and expensive. It meant that for much of the day, a data warehouse had low utilization. Historical data needed to be archived out of the data warehouse to keep backups manageable.

In the public cloud, the cost for computing is influenced by the size of the Virtual Machine (VM) and the length of time it is active (per second). The cost for storage is influenced by how much data needs to be persisted. The cheapest place to store data is object storage, which costs a few pennies per GB per month. Now, all of a company's data, say over 30 years' worth, can be stored cheaply on object storage. If reports for the past five years' worth of data need to be generated, a sufficient number of VMs can be started, the reports generated, and then the VMs shut down. Likewise for ETL. Costs are only incurred for the amount of time that the VMs are active. Because these clusters of compute are isolated from each other, it is possible for BI queries to run simultaneously as the ETL in the lakehouse without competing for resources.

The combination of public clouds and open source software has made open source projects enterprise-ready. Cloud managed services provide hosting, security, and scalability. Open source projects provide the critical capabilities and open Application Programming Interfaces (APIs). This has been a boon for companies with the ability to easily port workloads across providers and benefit from the secure environments and certifications of the cloud without needing to host the software themselves.

This is the perfect environment to build the unstructured portion of a lakehouse architecture.

An evolution to the open data lakehouse

Data management has evolved from analyzing structured data for historical analysis to making predictions using large volumes of unstructured data. There is an opportunity to leverage machine learning and a wider variety of datasets to unlock new value.

An open data lakehouse is necessary to provide the scalability and flexibility of a data lake with the performance and consistency of a data warehouse. The unstructured portion of the data lakehouse is built on top of open file formats, like Apache Parquet, which have already been adopted across a wide variety of tools.

Data can now be written to one place and have multiple open engines run against it. If one engine excels where another falters, companies can swap them as needed without expensive migrations. The open ecosystem developed around the unstructured portion of the data lakehouse ensures that adopters will have access to the latest innovations.

Whenever there is a widespread challenge in data management, it is typical for many different solutions to be developed to address it. This is true of proprietary software as well as open source projects. Equally, the market will eventually coalesce around one or two primary vendors or projects for a given technology space.

When an enterprise needs to vet a solution for their use case, open source has a clear advantage in measuring development velocity and adoption. A proprietary software vendor will rely on its marketing department to project leadership. Conversely, an open source project has features, bugs, commits, contributors, and releases happening in full public view. It is easy to measure the velocity of one open source project to another to see which one is garnering the most support and popularity.

All of the major cloud providers host the most popular open source projects and other third-party managed services. This provides customers with a choice to keep costs low and an incentive for each vendor to out-innovate each other.

The unstructured portion of the data lakehouse was born open. It is a culmination of open source software, open APIs, open file formats, and open tools. The pace of innovation in the community is remarkable, and new projects, such as data sharing, are being created quickly and in the open. Enterprises benefit from the open approach.

CHAPTER 5

Machine Learning and the Data Lakehouse

A previous chapter examined the role of the data warehouse for data scientists, who indeed have different requirements from typical end users. The data scientist is experimenting iteratively, looking for trends and performing statistical analysis, while end users typically run well-defined reports and visualize the result with business intelligence tools. The analytical infrastructure needs to support both.

The data scientist needs different tooling but has historically enjoyed some support from statistical environments like R, which can plug into data warehouses to retrieve data for work in a separate but suitable environment for data science.

Machine learning

A third analytical need has emerged for the unstructured portion of the data lakehouse: machine learning. The most visible example of machine learning is deep learning, which has achieved staggering results in image and text classification, machine translation, and self-driving cars. Deep learning's magic comes at a cost: it can require equally staggering amounts of compute with specialized hardware. High-quality machine learning models, which result from a learning process and can be used to make predictions, require huge amounts of data for training.

The good news is that the tools that power these techniques are open source, freely available, and constantly updated with cutting-edge ideas. The bad news is that these tools are not much like the traditional tools of the classic data warehouse and business intelligence environments. They aren't even much like data science tools.

This chapter will look at why machine learning is different and why the unstructured portion of the data lakehouse architecture was suited to its needs from the outset.

What machine learning needs from a lakehouse

While the work of a machine learning engineer or researcher overlaps with that of a data scientist, machine learning has distinguishing characteristics:

- operating on unstructured data like text and images
- requiring learning from massive data sets, not just analysis of a sample
- open source tooling to manipulate data as "DataFrames" (programming-language representations of tabular data) rather than with SQL commands
- outputs are models rather than data or reports

New value from data

It's essential to accommodate these users and use cases, as machine learning is a fountain of new potential ways to extract value from data in ways that weren't possible before. SQL-centric, table-centric, ETL-oriented architectures don't easily accommodate image or video files—these formats don't work well with pre-transforming, or ETLing, data into a table. Also, pulling huge data sets to a separate ML environment is costly, slow, and possibly insecure.

Resolving the dilemma

The unstructured portion of the data lakehouse paradigm resolves this dilemma by providing tools and data access to support these machine learning needs. The unstructured portion of the data lakehouse:

- Supports direct access to data as files in a variety of formats and "ELT" (Extract, Load, and Transform) in addition to "ETL"
- Supports in-place application of ML libraries on data in multiple languages, including Python and R
- Scales up not just SQL queries but the execution of ML tasks without exporting data

The following sections explore these ideas. To guide the discussion, consider a simplified data warehouse with an analytical environment architecture.

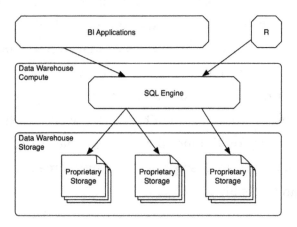

Figure 5-1. A simplified data warehouse with analytical environment architecture.

Compare this to a simple description of the unstructured portion of the data lakehouse architecture.

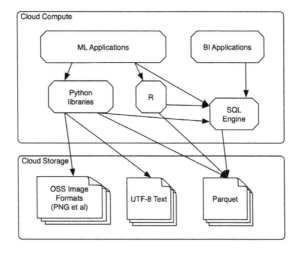

Figure 5-2. The unstructured portion of the data lakehouse architecture.

The problem of unstructured data

Machine learning, as a modern name for predictive modeling, isn't exactly new. However, the most visible gains from machine learning in the past decade have come in learning models from so-called 'unstructured' data. This typically refers to text, images, audio, or video data.

The term is misleading. All data has some structure. For example, text and images are just not tabular data, of the sort that data warehouses were built to manage. Now, it's fair to observe that some machine learning problems fit a data warehouse architecture. Sometimes the input data is simply tabular. Sometimes data sets aren't big. Sometimes data warehouses have custom database-specific support for building conventional models.

It's possible to treat these as simple text or binary types (TEXT, VARCHAR, BLOB) in a traditional data warehouse. However, this can have drawbacks:

- Storing huge BLOBs may not be supported or be inefficient
- Even if so, copying the data into a database may be slow and redundant
- Common open source tools are typically built to access files, not database tables

The idea of data as files is, of course, ancient. Any cloud provider like Amazon Web Services, Microsoft Azure, or Google Cloud Platform, is built on a bedrock of scale-out storage as 'files'. Previously, thinking of data as just files was an innovation—the so-called 'data lake' architecture from Apache Hadoop traded some of the data warehouse's advantages for easy, cheaper scale by generally only thinking of data as files.

A defining characteristic of the data lakehouse architecture is allowing direct access to data as files while retaining the valuable properties of a data warehouse. Just do both!

It's a trivial enough idea but something that conventional data warehouses assume isn't necessary. By hiding the storage, they can indeed implement some impressive optimizations. Yet, those optimizations are also possible when the architecture is built on open file formats in cloud storage—it's not mutually exclusive, just a legacy design decision.

In the unstructured portion of a data lakehouse, unstructured data can live happily in its natural form in standard file formats: UTF-8 text, JPEGs, MP4 videos, etc. This makes it far easier to apply the latest machine learning tools, which tend to expect unstructured data in this form.

The importance of open source

Open source tools are excellent and have large communities behind them that extend beyond any one organization or vendor. It's simply very hard to compete with the breadth and depth of the entire open source ecosystem. It's not reasonable to expect any single data warehouse to provide comparable functionality on its own, if it must reimplement this functionality to make it available directly within the data warehouse.

Even a venerable, mature standalone environment like R, open source and well-understood with a vibrant community, has not produced comparable functionality. These modern Python tools are the lingua franca of machine learning.

Machine learning users want to apply the skills they have and library tools they know. The unstructured portion of the data lakehouse architecture assumes the need to execute arbitrary libraries on data and expose data as files for those libraries. Therefore, it needs first-class support for managing and deploying libraries within the lakehouse.

In these respects, a good unstructured portion of the data lakehouse can and should feel like the same data and tool environment that machine learning users are accustomed to operating on a laptop. The data lakehouse also provides access to data-warehouse-like SQL functionality, security, and of course, scale.

Taking advantage of cloud elasticity

The allure of the cloud for data storage and compute lies in its near-infinite scale and cost-effectiveness. When more compute or storage is always available, scalability limits recede as a concern. Problems of under-provisioning and resource contention tend to vanish. This also means that over-provisioning worries recede. Because cost is driven only by usage, less is wasted on idling resources. These aren't new ideas, and newer data warehouse tools also benefit from cloud elasticity more than older statistically-sized architectures.

Scale is no good if it's not easily usable. The unstructured component of the data lakehouse architecture enables support for more general data access (files) and compute tools (Python, for example). While a lakehouse supports classic SQL-like workloads well at scale, it also needs to provide general scale-out compute support.

Machine learning workloads need to scale too, as the resulting models improve with more input. Several open-source tools, including Apache Spark, provide scale-out implementations of common model types.

Deep learning, however, has more specialized needs. Because of the scale and complexity of these models and their inputs, it's almost always beneficial to use specialized hardware to accelerate training. Unfortunately, data warehouse architectures typically do not assume specialized accelerators—they're expensive hardware and support ML use cases that don't fit the typical data warehouse design. In the cloud, these accelerators are available on-demand by the hour, however.

In the data lakehouse architecture, compute is transient and flexible. Machine learning jobs can provision accelerators from the cloud when needed without permanently providing them for all workloads. Open source tooling already knows how to utilize these devices. By making it easy to apply these tools to data, the lakehouse architecture makes it surprisingly easy to take advantage of cutting-edge deep learning ideas, which historically would have been prohibitive to develop outside of large tech companies like Google, Facebook, and Amazon.

Designing " MLOps" for a data platform

The rise of machine learning has created a new category of operations that a data architecture needs to support: so-called "MLOps." New needs arise as well: data versioning, lineage, and model management.

Models train on data, of course. It's important to track, sometimes for regulatory reasons, how a model was created and from what exact data. While it's possible to make copies of data sets when training models to record their input, this becomes infeasible at scale. Data sets may be large and expensive to copy, especially for every version of every model created. The unstructured component of data lakehouse architectures offers innovation in data storage that allows the efficient tracking of previous states of a dataset without copying.

Because models are closely related to the data they train on, it's also important to create them in the same place where the data lives, not in a separate environment. This helps optimize performance and improve operational concerns, like tracking which jobs are creating models and their overall lineage.

Finally, models are only useful if they can be applied to data. The outputs of ML workloads need to be first-class citizens in data architecture, on equal footing with other means of transforming data like with SQL.

The lakehouse architecture equally makes it natural to manage and apply models where the data lives.

Example: Learning to classify chest x-rays

Consider one example of a machine learning problem that easily fits the unstructured component of the data lakehouse architecture. The National Institute of Health released a dataset of 45,000 chest X-rays along with a clinician's diagnosis.[1] Today, it's entirely possible to learn, with some effectiveness, how to diagnose X-rays by

---

[1] https://www.nih.gov/news-events/news-releases/nih-clinical-center-provides-one-largest-publicly-available-chest-x-ray-datasets-scientific-community.

learning from a data set like this—or at least learn to explain what about the image suggests a diagnosis.

The possibilities are intriguing. It's not so much that a learned model will *replace* doctors and radiologists— although, in other tasks, deep learning has already achieved accuracies exceeding that of humans. Instead, it may *augment* their work. It may help catch subtle features of an X-ray that a human might miss in a diagnosis. It can help explain what it's "seeing" to a human as well—all with off-the-shelf software.

This section will summarize the ingredients of that solution within the unstructured component of the data lakehouse paradigm.

The data set consists of about 50GB of image data in 45,000 files along with CSV files containing clinical diagnoses for each file, which is simple enough to store cheaply in any cloud. The image files can be read directly into the unstructured component of the data lakehouse architecture, manipulated as if a table with open source tools, and further transformed in preparation for a deep learning tool. Likewise, the CSV files can be read directly as a table and joined with the images.

Deep learning is no simple task, but at least the software is well-understood and open source. Common choices of deep learning frameworks include PyTorch (from Facebook) and TensorFlow (from Google). The details of these libraries and their usage are beyond the scope of this book, but they are both designed to read image data from files, usually via standard open source tools, directly.

```
raw_image_df = spark.read.format("image").load("/mnt/databricks-datasets-private/ML/nih_xray/images/")
display(raw_image_df)
```

▶ (4) Spark Jobs

▶ 🔲 raw_image_df: pyspark.sql.dataframe.DataFrame = [image: struct]

Figure 5-3. The image files can be read directly into the unstructured component of the data lakehouse architecture.

The software needs hardware to run on, and lots of it. In the cloud, one can rent one machine, or a hundred, by the minute. They can include accelerators, and all major clouds offer a range of "GPUs" (graphics processing units), which are massively parallel devices for general large-scale number-crunching. Open source tools use these accelerators natively. The next step would be to provision one or more machines with accelerators in the cloud and simply run the learning software in-place in the cloud on the data. The result is a model encapsulating the learning achieved from these images.

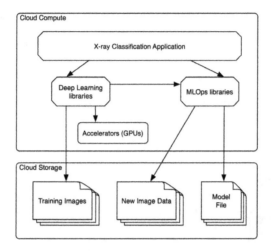

Figure 5-4. Provision one or more machines with accelerators in the cloud.

Given a chest X-ray image, the model can make plausible predictions of the doctor's diagnosis. With other open source tooling, it's possible to render human-readable explanations of its output.

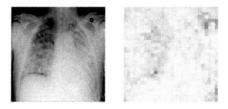

Figure 5-5. The model has produced a diagnosis of "Infiltration" with high confidence. The heatmap at the right shows regions of the image that are important to that conclusion. Darker regions are more important, and red ones support the conclusion while blue ones contradict it. Here, the artifact clearly present in the shoulder and lung were highlighted as important to a diagnosis of "Infiltration."

Finally, the model can be tracked with open source tools within a data lakehouse for lineage and reproducibility and later deployment of the model to production. Here's an example of one tool, MLflow, and what it automatically tracks about the learning process (a network architecture for example), to aid MLOps engineers in correctly setting up a service or batch job within the data lakehouse to apply the model to newly-arrived image files, perhaps streaming in to distributed storage in real-time.

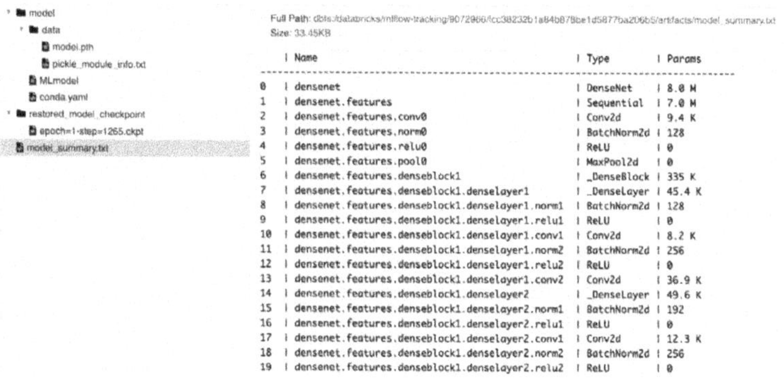

Figure 5-6. The model can be tracked with open source tools.

An evolution of the unstructured component

The unstructured component of the data lakehouse has evolved from the earlier versions of a data warehouse and data lake to offer the best of both worlds. In particular, the unstructured portion of the data lakehouse enables power ML use cases by:

- Leveraging standard open formats such as Apache Parquet to store data
- Allowing direct access to native data formats as files
- Enabling application of the vast world of open source libraries
- Powering in-place scale-out compute for large-scale modeling
- Enabling model management as a first-class concept via open source tools

CHAPTER 6

The Analytical Infrastructure for the Data Lakehouse

Once data was collected from applications. At first, this approach seemed to satisfy the end users. Then one day, the end users discovered that they needed data from more than one application at a time. An analytical infrastructure was needed to use the combined application data for analytical processing to accommodate this requirement.

Today, data is collected from an even wider and even more disparate set of data sources than a series of applications. That diverse set of data is placed in a data lake. Data is retrieved from applications, text, and other unstructured data such as analog and IoT data. Different technologies exist that make that collection of data into a data lake a reality. Those technologies include DataBricks, which collects structured and unstructured data, standard ETL, and Forest Rim textual ETL technology. These technologies collect and transform data into a form that the computer can analyze.

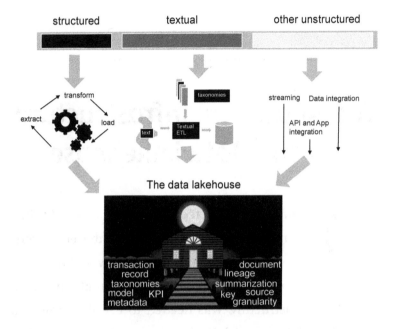

structured   textual   other unstructured

transform

taxonomies

extract   streaming   Data integration

load   API and App
integration

text   Textual
ETL

The data lakehouse

transaction   document
record   lineage
taxonomies   summarization
model   KPI   key   source
metadata   granularity

Figure 6-1. The collection of diverse types of data and the assimilation of that data into a data lake.

Collecting and assimilating the diverse amounts of data is its own difficult and important task. But after the data is gathered, it is discovered that merely gathering data into a data lake is not enough to facilitate the analysis of the data. To be useful, an analytical structure servicing the data lake is also needed. And if the data in the data lake cannot be analyzed and used, it is of little use.

Without the analytical infrastructure to accompany the data lake, the end user has difficulty navigating and interpreting the data found there. And if the end user has a difficult time using the facility, it won't be used. To accommodate the analytical usage of the data found in the data lake, it is necessary to create an analytical infrastructure for the data lake.

Once you combine the data lake along with analytical infrastructure, the entire infrastructure can be called a data lakehouse.

So what exactly does the analytical infrastructure of the data lake contain? What components are needed? And why are they needed?

Metadata

The first and most basic component needed for the analytical infrastructure is the metadata infrastructure. The metadata infrastructure allows the end user to find his/her way around the data lake. Metadata describes what data is in the data lake and how that data is structured. Metadata describes the naming conventions that are used and contains other descriptive metadata.

In many ways, the metadata for a data lake is like a giant roadmap as to what is in the data lake and where it lies. There are many different kinds of data in the data lake. For different types of data, there can be many different occurrences. As the data lake grows, more time is saved by quickly and accurately locating data.

Figure 6-2. Where do we find anything and what is it called?

The basic value of metadata is unquestioned. Suppose you want to drive from New York to Texas, but you have never before been out of the Bronx. If you just start driving, you may end up in Chicago. But if you want to get to Texas, your best bet is to get a map and figure which roads you need to take. You have greatly improved your odds of success by knowing where you are going before you start. Metadata plays the same role for the end user. If you want to do an analysis, it is really helpful to know what data you have to work with before you start analyzing.

The data model

One of the most important elements of metadata is the data model. The data model describes the general shape of the data found in the data lake and their relationship to each other. For example, the data model describes the cardinality of data, referential integrity, indexes, attributes, foreign keys, hierarchical relationships, and so forth. In addition, the data model describes all data found in the data lake, not just selected data in the data lake.

If the metadata is a map of the world, the data model is a map of Texas. A world map shows you how to get from England to Turkey, whereas the data model shows you how to get from El Paso to Houston.

There are many types of data from many different sources found in the data lake. To analyze data found in the data lake, it is a good idea to know what data is there and how the data relates to each other. There are data relationships inside a system and data relationships from data across multiple systems. To "see the big picture," it is useful to have data models that describe the data in the data lake.

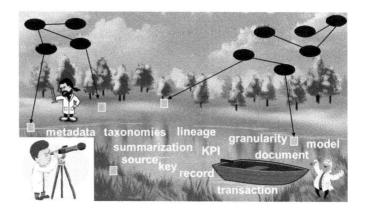

Figure 6-3. The data models reflect the contents and the relationships of the data in the data lake.

Data quality

Data arrives in the data lake in a wide variety of states. Some data is clean and vetted. Other data is merely taken from a source with no consideration of the data's reliability or veracity. For example, if data comes from a spreadsheet, there may be no veracity to the data at all. Therefore, before analytical activity can begin, there needs to be an assessment of the quality and reliability of the data found in the data lake.

Some of the elements of data quality include:

- Reliability
- Completeness
- Timeliness
- Consistency
- Veracity

It is dangerous to do an analysis and merge data with very different quality profiles. As a general rule, the veracity of merged data is only as good as the worst data that has been merged.

It is seen that a reliable picture of the quality and status of the data in the data lake is a useful thing to have. **Not knowing the quality of the data being analyzed jeopardizes the entire analysis.**

ETL

Another important element of the analytical infrastructure is ETL. ETL transforms application data for analysis. For example, suppose you have data about money from the US, Australia, and Canada. All three currencies are in dollars. But you can't just add the dollars together and have a meaningful answer. Instead, to have a meaningful answer, you have to convert (transform) two of the three currencies to a common value. Then, and only then, can you add the values up in a meaningful manner.

And even then, the truthfulness of the data is only relevant to the moment that data has been recalculated because exchange rates fluctuate on a daily/hourly basis.

There are many such transformations of data needed inside the data lake. Currency exchange is merely one of thousands of necessary data transformations.

Data is reshaped into a common format by the passage of the data through ETL processing.

The end user needs to know about the data transformations that have occurred in the data lake.

There are many different types of data transformations. Application data can be transformed into corporate data by ETL. Raw text can be transformed into a database format by textual ETL. Other unstructured data can go through segmentation and data reduction.

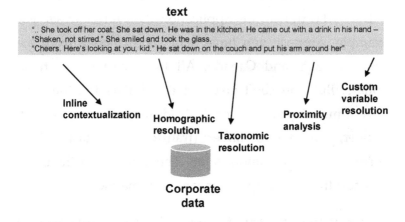

Figure 6-4. It is useful to know what type of transformation has occurred before the data arrives in the data lake.

Textual ETL

Similar to ETL is textual ETL. Textual ETL performs the same transformation of data as does ETL. The difference is that textual ETL operates on raw text whereas ETL operates on structured application-based data. Raw text is read into textual ETL and a database containing both words and context is returned. Once text has been reduced to a database format, it can be analyzed along with other types of data.

The end user needs to understand what transformations have been made and what data is available for analysis after the textual ETL process has been run to do proper analytics. Textual ETL is quite different from standard structured application ETL. As such, it is useful to describe the processes that textual ETL has gone through to create the textual data found in the data lake.

Taxonomies

One of the essential ingredients of textual transformation is that of taxonomies. Taxonomies are to raw text what the data model is to structured application data. Taxonomies are used in the transformation of raw text into a database. Taxonomies have a great influence on the way textual transformation is accomplished. Both the quality and quantity of transformation greatly influence the taxonomies used by textual ETL.

In many ways, taxonomies are to textual ETL what the data model is to standard ETL. Consequently, the taxonomies used in textual ETL greatly affect the quality and accuracy of the transformation accomplished by textual ETL. Therefore, it is useful to have the taxonomies available for inspection when examining the data in the data lake.

Figure 6-5. How can structure be added to text?

Volume of data

The volume of data in the data lake can be a significant factor when the end user constructs a plan for analytics. Some data can be accessed and analyzed in its entirety and other data needs to be sampled before it is analyzed. The end user needs to be aware of these factors. The analytics infrastructure needs to have this information readily and easily available.

The volume of data plays a big role in the usage and transformation on data. Small volumes of data can be manipulated with agility, whereas large volumes of data are much less agile in their ability to be manipulated. In some cases, the sheer volume of data found in the data lake is greatly impacted by the volume of data. This is especially true for other unstructured data such as analog data and IoT data.

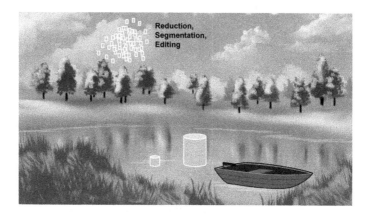

Figure 6-6. If accommodations have to be made for the volume of data, this accommodation is a necessary part of the analytical infrastructure.

Lineage of data

Another important piece of analytical information about data in the data lake that the end user needs is data lineage. It is normal for data to be ingested at one point and then transformed at another point. Throughout the life of the data, there may be a long string of transformations. On occasion, the end user needs to see the origins of data and what transformations have been made. By understanding the data lineage, the end user can accurately determine what data is best to use in any given analysis.

This disclosure of the data lineage is an important part of the analytical infrastructure for the data lake. In an earlier day and age, the lineage of data was clear, apparent, and simple. But as organizations have grown larger and older and IT organizations have grown, the data lineage has grown more complex. Unfortunately, for many types of analysis, the lineage of data is an important issue—a very important issue. There needs to be a clear and incontrovertible description of the data found in the data lake for the data to be accurately analyzed.

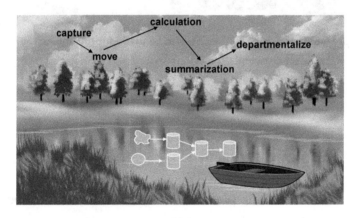

Figure 6-7. The lineage of data.

KPIs

KPIs (Key Performance Indicators) are probably the most important indicators the end user can provide the organization. Usually, KPIs are calculated on a periodic basis—weekly, monthly, etc. Often the KPIs are calculated from application data. Other times KPIs are created from other types of data. KPIs usually are stored in long-term storage. Occasionally it behooves the organization to take a historical look at its KPIs. When the KPIs are clearly designated and stored in the data lake, it is easy for the end user to find the KPIs and facilitate analysis. It is normal for there to be many KPIs scattered throughout the data lake. The world goes into a panic when it comes time to find a specific KPI. There is always the chance that you don't have the correct KPI. Or the most up-to-date KPI. Or that there is a better KPI.

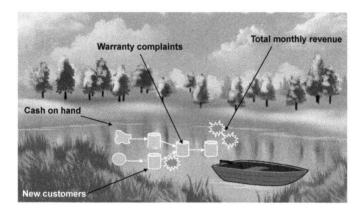

Figure 6-8. One of the most important features of analysis in the data lake is the quick and accurate ability to find the KPI you need.

Granularity

One of the key data and analytical features in the data lake is the granularity of data. If data is not granular enough, it cannot support a flexible analytical pattern. On the other hand, if the data is too granular, the data consumes too much space. In addition, when the data is too granular, it becomes unwieldy to handle. Furthermore, suppose the granularity of data is different for two or more stores of data. In that case, the differences between the granularity of data impede the ability of the end user to do his/her work.

To do analytics properly, the end user must be aware of the granularity of the data found in the data lake.

Perhaps the most basic measurement of data that affects its ability to be compared and integrated to other data is that of the granularity of data. Consequently, there needs to be a clear and concise definition of the different levels of granularity of the data found in the data lake.

Transactions

Some but not all data is generated by transactions. In some cases, the transactions themselves are stored in the data lake. If that is the case, it makes sense for the transactions to be documented to the point that they are readily available for the end user when examining the data lake.

Many forms of analysis require the end user to refer back to the transactions that have transpired.

There are many types of data found in the organization. But the type of data most directly affecting the organization is usually its transactions. As a consequence, it makes sense to identify where those transactions reside in the data lake.

Keys

A special form of metadata is keys. Keys form the identifiers through which data can readily be located. Therefore, keys should be identified and made available for efficient access to the data lake.

Keys are necessary to understand the very fabric of the data found in the data lake. Stated differently, if you don't understand the keys to the data lake, you will have a hard time analyzing data.

Keys are the lifeblood of understanding what is in the data lake. With keys, you can locate any occurrence of data. With keys, you can determine how two different types of data can be related. With keys you can start to understand the structure of the data.

Keys play a vital role in the building of the analytical infrastructure of the data lake.

Schedule of processing

Data enters the data lake from many different sources and in many different ways. Therefore, there needs to be a "timeclock" to enter data into the data lake. When there is a data timeclock, the end user can know when data has arrived in the lake.

On occasion, the end user needs to know when data entered the system, when it was processed, and so forth. In many ways, it seems trivial to consider when data was last updated or refreshed. But when you start to do analytics on data, the data and its "freshness" greatly impact the analysis that can be done.

As a consequence, the schedule of refreshment of data in the data lake becomes an important feature of the data lake.

Summarizations

Some data in the lake is detailed data and some data is summarized. For the summarized data, there needs to be documentation of the algorithm used to create the summarization and a description of the selection process of the summarized data. The end user needs to know what data has been selected for summarization and what data has not been selected for summarization.

This documentation of summarizations is necessary for the succinct analysis of the data found in the lake. The data lake is often full of summarizations. Looking at summarizations can save huge amounts of time, rather than going back to the raw data and recalculating the summarized data. However, summarizations carry with them two important considerations:

- What data was chosen for the summarization process?
- What algorithm was used to create the summarization?

So there are three characteristics of summarizations needed for the analytical infrastructure:

- What summarizations are there?
- How was the summarization calculated?
- What data was chosen for the summarization?

Figure 6-9. What summarizations are done and what algorithms are used?

Minimum requirements

There are a set of minimum requirements for data in the lake to be easily and accurately analyzed.

To understand the value of the analytical infrastructure, consider the process of doing analytics without the analytical infrastructure. When there is no analytical infrastructure, the end user spends his/her time trying to either find or "clean up" the data, not doing analysis. The analytical infrastructure is derived solely and entirely from the data that resides in the data lake.

The data lake without the analytical infrastructure simply becomes a data swamp. And a data swamp does no one any good.

CHAPTER 7

Blending Data in the Data Lakehouse

One of the characteristics of most computing and analytical environments is that the environment consists of only one type of data. For example, the OLTP environment consists primarily of transaction-based data. The data warehouse environment consists of integrated, historical data. The textual environment consists of text, and so forth.

The lakehouse and the data lakehouse

There is an exception to the singularity of types of data when it comes to the data lakehouse. The data lakehouse consists of essentially three types of data—structured, transaction-based data, textual data, and other unstructured data such as IoT and analog-based data. Because of this fundamental mixture of different types of data found in the data lakehouse, a new problem is introduced when using the data lakehouse for analytics.

That problem arises in blending the different types of data together in a cohesive manner.

To do analytical processing using blended data, the end user must address how to analyze data emanating from several different environments.

The origins of data

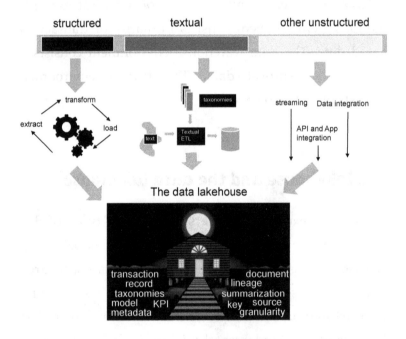

Figure 7-1. The origins of the data found in the data lakehouse.

Data in the data lakehouse is created from three different processing technologies. Structured data and other unstructured data in the lake are received from technology such as Databricks. Textual data enters after passing raw text through technology such as textual ETL. And other unstructured data arrives in the data lakehouse by means of data reduction, data segmentation, and other statistical processes. From these sources of data, the data lakehouse is built.

Different types of analysis

Once in the data lakehouse, there are essentially two types of analysis to perform.

One type of analysis is the analysis of singular environments—analysis of *only* the structured environment, analysis of *only* the textual environment, and analysis of the *only* other unstructured environment. Analysis in the structured environment consists of looking for KPIs and so forth. Analysis in the other unstructured environment consists of trend and pattern analysis. The analysis of singular environments is not new and has been around for a long time.

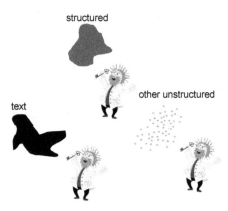

Figure 7-2. Each environment is analyzed separately.

The other type of analysis is the analysis of blended environments—analysis of the structured and the textual environment, analysis of the structured environment and the other unstructured environment, and analysis of the other unstructured environment and the textual environment.

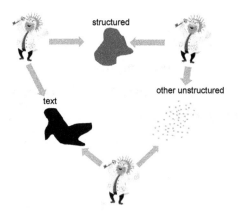

Figure 7-3. Analyzing multiple environments.

In the case of structured and textual data, the data is easily matched because both environments are in a standard database format. However, blending in the data from the other unstructured environment is a bit more difficult because the data from that environment may not be in a compatible format.

But data format is only the tip of the iceberg. An even more perplexing problem is the problem of finding common information across the different environments.

The structured environment is the easiest environment to address. Its data is already in the format of keys, records, and attributes. Under most circumstances, the keys and terms found in the structured environment are only randomly found in the textual environment. In some cases, the textual environment may have keys and other attributes. But in most cases, there is no uniformity of data found in the textual environment. The other unstructured environment is also bereft of keys. There may or may not be keys in the other unstructured environment.

Common identifiers

The problem is that to do analytical processing across different environments, it is necessary to have some common basis for comparison. The good news is that there are such things as common identifiers for any environment. Some of those common identifiers across multiple environments are:

- Time
- Geography
- Money
- Names
- Events

Structured identifiers

Data in the structured environment is typically found in a highly structured fashion (as you might expect).

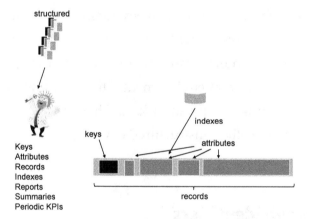

Figure 7-4. The structured environment contains keys, attributes, indexes, and records.

Each record in the structured environment has all of these characteristics. A key might be Social Security Number, attributes might be a person name or phone number, an index might be the town a person lives in—all of this information exists in a single record.

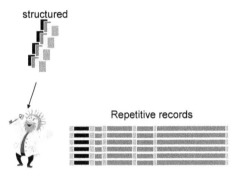

Figure 7-5. Each record in the structured environment has all of this information.

Repetitive data

Because each record in the structured environment has the same type of information, the records are said to be repetitive. Having the same *type of* information in each record does not mean that the same information is in each record. In one record, the name might be Mary Jones. In the next record, the name is Sam Smith. But in each record there will be a name.

There is a difference between the same type of data and the same data.

When a person is doing analytical processing against structured data exclusively, one typical kind of processing is looking for KPIs. Usually, KPIs are found in a periodic basis and the performance from one period of time to the next is tracked and compared.

As a simple example of the analysis that can be created from structured data only, the end user may issue a monthly report about cash flow. Cash comes from different sources and varies from month to month. The analysis of the cash flow is one of the KPIs of the organization.

Identifiers from the textual environment

Data from the textual environment starts out as raw text. The raw text can come from almost anywhere. The raw text may come from emails, the Internet, surveys, conversations, printed reports, and so forth. Once the raw text is captured and placed into a format where it can be read and managed, the raw text is then transformed into a database. It is necessary to transform the data into a database because if analytical processing is to be done on blended data, the data must be structured into a database.

If text is left in a raw textual format, it does not fit into a database in a useful manner.

There are several elements that the database resulting from transforming text needs:

- Identification of the originating document
- Location of the word of interest in the document being analyzed
- The word of interest
- The context of the word of interest

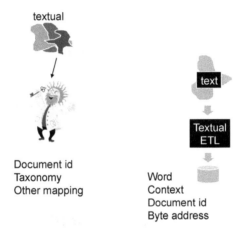

Figure 7-6. Identifiers from the textual environment.

As an example of the kinds of data that might be found in the textual environment, Document id might be "YELP Comment 506 on Jan 27, 2020," Byte address might be "byte 208," Word might be "liked," and Context might be "positive sentiment."

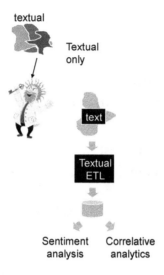

Figure 7-7. You can do either sentiment analysis or correlative analysis if you are doing analytic processing exclusively using raw text as a basis for analysis.

Combining text and structured data

The most powerful kind of combined analytical processing that you can do is combine the data from both the structured and textual environments. To do this kind of analysis, we must join the data from the two environments together.

From a format perspective, combining the two types of data is easy to do. But there is more to combining data than the mere merging of the format of the data.

As an example of a join of data from the textual environment and the structured environment, consider the comment, "I am really disappointed in my recent purchase of a Chevrolet." When the customer comment is matched with the purchase records, it is seen that the customer bought a Chevrolet Camaro brand new in 2007. So now, the comment can be attached to a specific automobile.

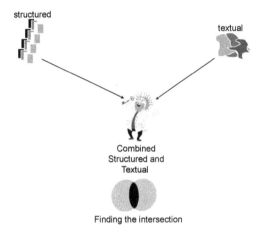

structured

textual

Combined
Structured and
Textual

Finding the intersection

Figure 7-8. The most interesting data (and the most useful for analytics) is the data where there is an intersection of the different kinds of data.

Finding an intersection of data is often difficult because of the fundamental differences between the two types.

Textual data has an identifier

The easiest way to meaningfully blend data from the two environments is when the textual data has an identifier associated with the data. In many forms of textual data, a specific identifier does exist and can be found. A typical identifier might be a Social Security Number, a passport number in a document, or an employee number. On occasion, the document itself requires some form of identification.

If there is an identifier in the textual document, then matching the textual document with the structured document becomes fairly straightforward.

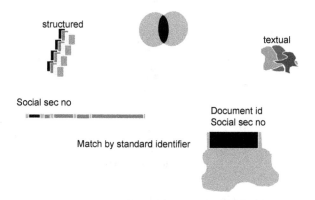

structured

textual

Social sec no

Document id
Social sec no

Match by standard identifier

Figure 7-9. The Social Security Number in the structured environment is matched to the same Social Security Number in the textual document.

Note that some raw text documents have a component that is structured. If that is the case, then matching structured data and unstructured data becomes easy to do.

But many textual documents have neither a structured component nor an identifier. In this case, it is possible to find other data types on which to blend.

Date as an identifier

Another simple way to blend documents is to find dates in both structured and unstructured data.

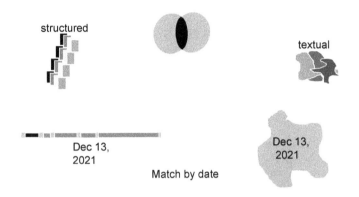

Figure 7-10. It is very common for both types of documents to have some form of date.

Note that there are lots of different kinds of dates. There is purchase date, manufacture date, sales date, date of data capture, and so forth. The most meaningful type of date is typically one that reflects the date of the transaction, if there happens to be a transaction involved.

A mechanical consideration in matching dates is matching the different forms of representation that text might take. For example, in one case date may be March 13, 2021, and in another case, the data may be 3/13/2021. Logically these are the same date. But physically, they are very different. So it is necessary to convert the date formats into a common format.

Location (geography) as an identifier

Another way to match the different types of data is by location (or geography). As a simple example, the state of Texas may be found in both types of documents—the structured document and the textual document. A match can be made on the name or other designation of the state. A mechanical consideration is that state name can take more than one form.

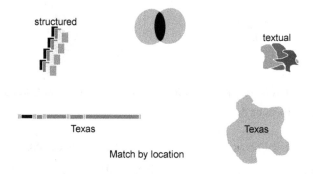

Figure 7-11. In one case, Texas may be spelled out as 'Texas.' In another document, the state can be abbreviated as 'TX.' In yet another form, Texas may appear as 'Tex.'

Person name as an identifier

Yet another way that data can be blended is on the name itself. In the example shown, the name "Jena Smith" is found in documents in the structured environment and documents found in the textual environment.

Matching on names is the weakest form of matching that there is, since:

- Name can be spelled many ways—J Smith, Jena Smith, J H Smith, etc.
- More than one person may have the same name
- A person may or may not use a title—Mr., Mrs., Ms., Dr., etc.

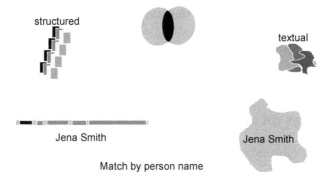

Figure 7-12. As a general rule, matches on names should not be considered to be a match made in concrete. Stated differently, matching on names leads to questionable results.

Product name as an identifier

Yet another way that structured and textual documents can be blended is by the matching of product names. For example, a product known as the "4x2 Television" can be matched across different environments.

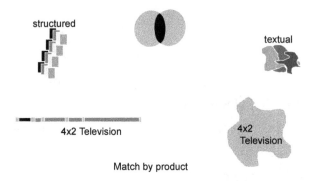

Figure 7-13. The problem with this matching approach is that the same product can be named slightly differently in multiple places.

Money as an identifier

Another common identifier is money.

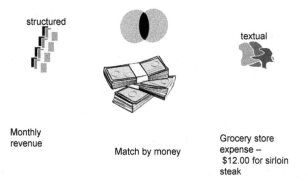

Figure 7-14. Money exists in both the structured environment and the textual environment. For this reason, money can be used as a common identifier across different environments.

But there are some problems with money. The first problem is the consistency of the currency of the money.

You should not be comparing the Mexican peso to the Chilean peso unless you have made the appropriate conversion. And if you have converted the money, you need to specify the conversion date because the conversion rate changes over time.

The second difficulty with money being used as a basis for comparison is that the actual value of money changes over time due to inflation. Comparing dollars from 1926 to dollars from 2010 produces a very distorted comparison, even when the currency stays the same.

Nevertheless, in some cases, dollar values from the different environments can be successfully used as a basis of comparison.

The importance of matching

It may not be obvious, but there is great value in matching structured data and text. The value lies in the matching criterion determining how the analysis and comparison between the two environments can be conducted.

Because the criterion for matching the two environments determines how your analysis can be done, it is very important to consider how your data is matched.

Imperfect matching

Regardless of how the data matching is done, there is always the chance that some documents will not have a corresponding match. In other words, there will be documents in the structured world that match with nothing in the text world. And vice versa. There will be documents in the textual world that will have no match in the world of structured data. As an example, a person buys a car but never renders an opinion of the car. In this case, there will be a structured record of the purchase of the car but no textual opinion of the car. Such mismatches are common and create no cause for concern.

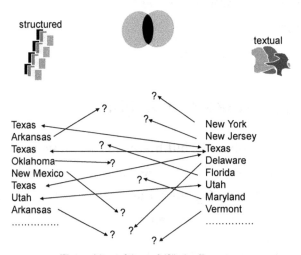

The problem of the unfulfilled references

Figure 7-15. It simply is inevitable that there will be some of this mismatch of the documents and data to each other. The sources of data were never designed to be tightly coordinated, so it is no surprise that not all data is matched.

Matching other unstructured data to structured or textual data

The matching of other unstructured data to other types of data faces the same issues as the other forms of matching data. Data can be matched on time, geography, names, and/or money.

Usually, some form of structured reference is available from the world of other unstructured data. However, the data in this world tends to be very voluminous and singularly non-robust.

CHAPTER 8

Types of Analysis Across the Data Lakehouse Architecture

The many different kinds of queries and analyses using the three types of data in the data lakehouse can be grouped into two categories:

1. Queries and analysis where the results are known before the query is issued or are anticipated at the start of the query

2. Queries and analysis where the results of the query process are unknown at the start

Known queries

In the case of known result type queries, the requirements for processing are known at the outset. For the most part, these types of queries and analyses involve merely searching for data. On occasion, some light amount of calculation is required after having found the data.

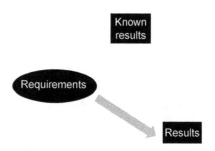

Figure 8-1. In the case of known result type queries, the requirements for processing are known at the outset.

As an example of a known query, suppose a person walks into a bank and wants to know their account balance. The bank teller finds the account number, enters a query, and then tells the person that they have $3,208.12 in their account. This is current and accurate information. The hardest part about this query is in finding the correct data.

How much money is in
my account right now?

"$3208.12"

Figure 8-2. In this case, the query merely requires that the person's account balance be identified. Then a search is made and the information is located.

A more complex example of a known query is the case where a manager wants to know how much cash is available right now for the business across multiple accounts. Furthermore, the manager wants to see how the calculation of cash on hand stacks up over time. In this case, it is required to:

- Find available cash from all sources and add them together
- Find this value monthly for the preceding six months or so

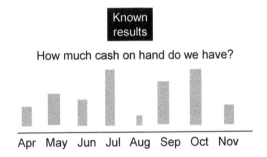

Figure 8-3. In this case, merely finding a unit of data is the first step. After all the data is found, then some amount of calculation is required.

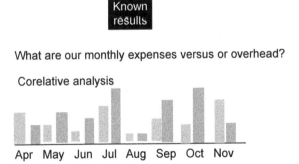

Figure 8-4. A more sophisticated type of analysis compares cash on hand to the monthly amount of expenses.

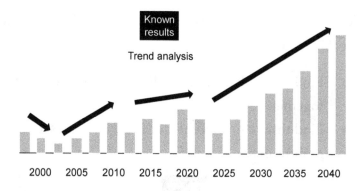

Figure 8-5. And this form of analysis can be combined to create a larger trend analysis.

Heuristic analysis

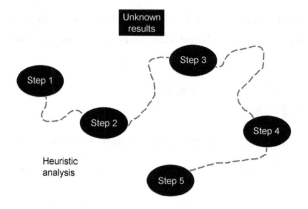

Figure 8-6. Another form of analysis is the type of analysis where it is not known that results are available. In fact, it is often the case that no one knows if there are even any results to be found. This type of analysis is known as heuristic analysis.

Heuristic analysis is sometimes called "exploration analysis." In heuristic analysis, the next step of analysis depends on the results of the previous step. When a person starts to do heuristic analysis, it is not clear how long the analysis will take, how many steps there might be, and even if a final result can be found or calculated.

One form of heuristic analysis is the finding of a needle in a haystack. Suppose an end user wants to find if there is a bank customer who is working for a competitor. There may or may not be such an individual. Or there may be more than one such person.

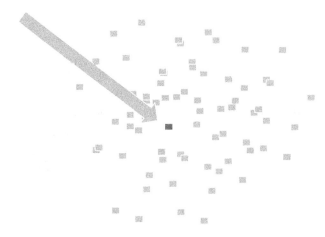

Figure 8-7. The search starts to find one or more customers who fit this criterion

But searching for a single needle in the haystack is not the only kind of heuristic analysis to do. Another type of analysis is that of looking for a pattern among a lot of records.

Finding the pattern in a crowded field

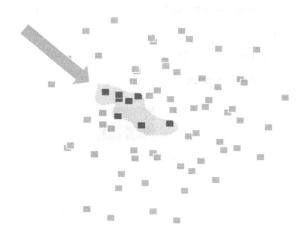

Figure 8-8. Suppose the end user wanted to find if patients who had died from COVID were significantly overweight. Or what other characteristics did patients have who had passed away because of COVID? There may or may not be multiple patients who fit this criterion. The search for a pattern commences.

Part of the process of doing heuristic analysis is that of recognizing and removing outliers. In a large body of outcomes, there are always some units of data to discount.

Recognizing and identifying outliers

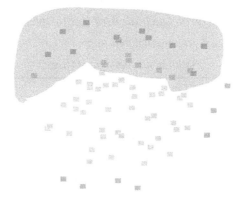

Figure 8-9. The end user wishes to discard patient records where the patient has been in treatment for more than three days. These records are located and removed.

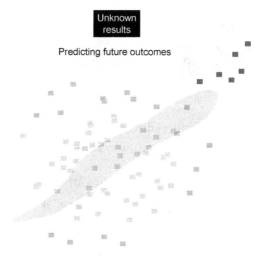

Figure 8-10. The the most useful form of heuristic analysis is making future predictions. Future predictions are based on the recurrence of the same conditions producing the same or otherwise predictable results in the future.

The different types of data found in the data lakehouse lend themselves to different types of processes and analyses. Structured data works best for known analysis and queries. Other unstructured data lends itself best to unknown queries and analyses. And textual data supports both known and unknown types of analytics.

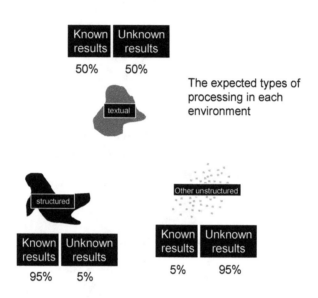

Figure 8-11. The propensity of different data types found in the data lakehouse supports different query and analysis types.

Because of the different proclivities of the different types of data for different types of processing, it is only natural that there is a different success rate in combining the different types of data.

It is seen that textual data combines well with structured data and other unstructured data, while there is only minimal interaction between structured data and other unstructured data.

There is a poor track record in combining structured data with other unstructured data.

To do the combination of these different types of data it is necessary to use universal connectors.

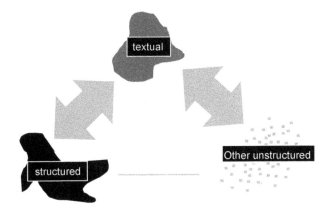

Figure 8-12. Blending the different types of data found in the data lake.

CHAPTER 9

Data Lakehouse Housekeeping™

W here there is a house, there is housekeeping. The moment we talk about a house, the first thing that comes to mind is, "What does the house look like?" Then, you start imagining its exterior, interior, layout, design, aesthetics, lot size, connecting roads, architecture, and many more things that a human being can imagine about a house.

Once the house is built, you can't leave the house abandoned. An abandoned house starts looking like a haunted house after few years or a decade. Therefore, to maintain a beautifully built or constructed house, we need excellent housekeeping. Housekeeping will keep the house maintained and in order by managing regular household affairs. Excellent and regular housekeeping will make the residents' stay in the house enjoyable, leading to the residents' happiness and delight year after year.

Housekeeping in terms of an organization means recordkeeping which facilitates productive work in an organization.

Similar is the case with a data lakehouse. We need to set up the housekeeping processes in place for a data lakehouse to be a data lakehouse forever, or else it becomes a data lake (like a haunted house in the above example). "Data Lakehouse Housekeeping" will help keep the data lakehouse in order year over year.

Data lakehouse housekeeping helps maintain and keep the data lakehouse in order year over year.

Please remember that the housekeeping process establishes the strong distinction between a data lake and data lakehouse. As we know, a data lakehouse brings in the best of both data warehouse and data lake. It helps you maintain the hygiene of the lakehouse. This housekeeping will help the data lakehouse maintain its identity year over year and not become a data swamp or a data lake.

It is the process of housekeeping that can help you establish a data lakehouse from a data lake.

The housekeeping of the data lakehouse will help maintain the standard data acquisition, transformation, federation, and extraction processes. It also helps regulate data management and governance in the lakehouse.

Data lakehouse housekeeping will make a data lakehouse a data lakehouse—else it is simply a data lake.

Once you think of a data lakehouse, what kind of housekeeping can keep the data lakehouse in order? Is it by managing all data-related household affairs within the lakehouse? In terms of data lakehouse housekeeping, examples of questions to address are:

- How will the data be integrated within the data lakehouse?
- How ~~much~~ interoperable should it be?
- How can we manage the master reference within the data lakehouse?
- How can we manage the single version of the truth?
- What privacy and confidentiality measures need to be considered and applied within the data lakehouse?
- How can we make sure that the data is relevant and usable, even decades in the future?
- How do we do data lakehouse routine maintenance?

Technically a data lakehouse without data lakehouse housekeeping is only the data lake. We dump the source

data as is by following standard data lake creation
processes.

---

*To combine the robustness of a data warehouse with the
capabilities of a data lake into a data lakehouse, we need
disciplined and meticulous data lakehouse housekeeping.*

Data integration and interoperability

Data integration and data interoperability include:

- Data acquisition
- Data extraction
- Data transformation
- Data movement
- Data replication
- Data federation

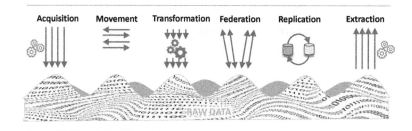

Figure 9-1. Aspects of data integration and data interoperability in a
Data Lakehouse.

Data acquisition

Data acquisition includes but is not limited to converting the physical condition of data into a digital and structured form for further storage and analysis. Typically, IoT data also includes signals from sensors, voice, text, Textual ETL outputs, logs, and many more sources. A data lakehouse is designed to store IoT data.

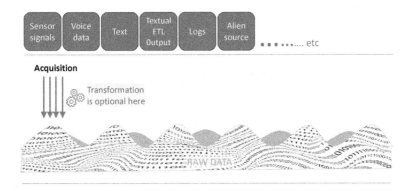

Figure 9-2. Data Acquisition from heterogeneous sources in a data lakehouse.

After acquisition, the transformation is optional and subject to format differences before dumping the data into the data lakehouse.

Data extraction

Data extraction is the first step in any data ingestion process.

Data extraction is the process of extracting data from databases or software as a service platform, including any architecture pattern like the data lake or data lakehouse.

The extraction happens in both directions. After acquiring the data, you extract the source data to the data lake. And there are lots of architectural patterns that need to be applied to call that data lake a data lakehouse. We can then extract data from the data lakehouse for various consumption purposes.

Data extraction is the first step in the data ingestion process. The data ingestion process can be either ETL or ELT. 'Extract' is the first step in both processes.

Data transformation

Data transformation is the process of mapping and converting data from one format to another. Data transformation is needed when you expect data from heterogeneous sources due to different data formats from across sources. This transformed format is nothing but the uniform format decided for the data lakehouse. Data transformation is a component of almost all data integration and management activities, including data warehousing and data lakehouse creation.

Data transformation takes place in almost all data integration and data management activities.

Data transformation is needed in a data lakehouse when integrating heterogeneous sources like XML, XLS, Word, text, PDF, RDBMS, textual ETL outputs, CSVs, and flat files. Transformation can also be for bidirectional purposes, including inbound and outbound from the data lake.

Transformation is even required internally as well when it comes to data lakehouse formation, because data lakehouse frameworks transform the data from the data lake.

Hence transformation is needed when the data needs to be mapped due to data format differences or source-to-destination file or storage format differences. In s few cases, it might be simple and straightforward. In another case, it might be complex, requiring potential changes to the data and its format before it reaches the destination file or storage format and is stored for successful hassle-free uses.

Transformation is needed whenever and wherever there are format differences, and the data between source and destination needs a strategic mapping with appropriate transformation rules.

Three things are important to decide whether the data needs any transformation before storing it in the target file format. First is the source data format understanding, second is the desired data format expected into the destination, and third is the transformation logic to be applied to bring the difference to an acceptable format into the final destination file and storage data format.

Master references for the data lakehouse

Why master references in a data lakehouse? A data lakehouse is not a data lake. In a data lake, you might not need a master reference. But as we have learned, a data lakehouse is the best of both data warehouse and data lake. Hence, a managed master reference becomes obvious. A master reference is the reference of master data to manage shared data to reduce redundancy and ensure better data quality through standardized definition and data values. It helps maintain a single version of the truth across systems.

A distinction between shared and distinct data across the organization is very important in data lakehouse housekeeping. It helps you build the master reference.

Figure 9-3. The master reference layer in a data lakehouse.

Earmarking such shared data will help maintain a single version of the truth across the data lakehouse. A data lakehouse is not the dumping yard. At one end, it will store data from heterogeneous sources. At another end, it will be the source of truth for various external but dependent systems. Various enterprise systems might extract required data periodically or regularly from the data lakehouse. In some cases, the data lakehouse might be the direct source of data for a few enterprise applications, including but not limited to various analytics, data science, or cognitive tools/applications.

> *The data lakehouse can be a source of truth for various external systems within or outside an enterprise.*

Once master reference earmarking is over, the layer needs to be structured and brought into use. Every system or segment of data within and outside the data lakehouse (consumers of data lakehouse) should rely only on the reference and master data designed for the purpose. It must be part of all ETL happening over the data lakehouse.

Next comes the question of precedence of references for master data. This is a very natural question and it has solutions already existing and used almost everywhere to create any master information repository. Product owners or functional experts decide the precedence of data to overwrite and/or update a data into reference data or the master data store. And application engineers need to write the rule engine that needs to be followed for any master data overwrite/update or even delete (a soft or physical delete).

For example, an enterprise has many applications that capture a customer address. It might be captured in a CRM, a sales application, and a finance or billing application. All applications might have captured the same customer's address differently. The CRM might have captured its customer's address as 'Sector – 53, Gurgaon, India.' The sales application might have an older address from this same customer, 'Chanakyapuri, New Delhi.' But today, this customer is staying in 'Bangalore, India,' and the billing has the latest updated address.

So, once an enterprise has a master reference, all applications will rely upon that single version of truth. And for the first creation of that single version of the truth, the precedence rule needs to be written that says which address will go and sit in the master reference. And here in this example, it should be the billing application address that is the most current.

Data lakehouse privacy, confidentiality, and data protection

Data privacy, data confidentiality, and data protection are
sometimes incorrectly diluted with security.

For example, data privacy is related to, but not the same as, data security. Data security is concerned with assuring the confidentiality, integrity, and availability of data. Data privacy focuses on how and to what extent businesses may collect and process information about individuals.

You can say that privacy needs security (there is no privacy without security), but security doesn't need privacy. A data lakehouse must maintain data privacy and data confidentiality with data protection.

Data privacy, interchangeably called information privacy, often refers to a specific kind of privacy linked to personal information provided to private actors in various contexts. Here the definition of personal information is very subjective and may be defined differently in different contexts and domains. For example, personal information on social media might be your personal credentials, including name, sex, age, address, contact number, ethnicity, and so on. Personal information in healthcare might include vital EMR attributes like diagnosis, health conditions, vitals, treatments, and so on.

Data confidentiality deals with protecting against the disclosure of information by ensuring that the data is limited to those authorized, or by representing the data in such a way that its actual or original value remain accessible only to those who are entitled or possess some critical information (e.g. a decryption or decoding key for an encrypted or coded data).

For example, a patient was diagnosed with AIDS. But the patient might not be interested in sharing his/her medical condition or the diagnosis of AIDS to anyone except his/her doctor who is treating him/her. Hence it is the hospital's accountability to maintain the confidentiality of the data of that specific patient. The application used to capture and store his/her data should be capable of handling this confidentiality. These data confidentiality rules apply to the data lake or data lakehouse where that data ultimately resides.

Data protection is the process of safeguarding important data or information from corruption, compromise, or loss. The definition of *importance* can be different for different entities or organizations. Important data can be unpublished financial information, customer data, patents, formulas or new proprietary technologies, pricing strategies, etc. Hence, the data protection process should be robust enough and comprehensive enough to address all such required data protection to defined enterprise data.

A few commonly known data or information privacy, confidentiality, and protection policies are:

- The Health Insurance Portability and Accountability Act (HIPAA)
- The Family Educational Rights and Privacy Act (FERPA)
- The Children's Online Privacy Protection Act (COPPA)
- The Gramm-Leach-Bliley Act (GLBA)
- The European Union's General Data Protection Regulation (GDPR)
- The California Consumer Privacy Act (CCPA)

When you do the housekeeping of a data lakehouse, have a data protection process for privacy policies, applicable confidentiality rules, and regulations. As mentioned, it is very subjective and may be defined differently in different contexts.

Act responsibly while dealing with data privacy and confidentiality in a data lakehouse architecture pattern. Remember that a data lakehouse is very much part of the enterprise system. The data privacy, confidentiality, and data protection rules should be more comprehensively applied to a data lake or data lakehouse because a data lakehouse will accommodate data from hundreds or thousands of applications.

While housekeeping a data lakehouse, awareness of the applicable data privacy and confidentiality rules and a robust data protection process is essential.

"Data future-proofing™" in a data lakehouse

In terms of data, 'future-proofing' can be defined as the process of anticipating the future and developing methods of capturing and arranging the data in a way that can minimize the gap due to missing data or irrelevant data, for the future purpose of relevant data driven researches, correlations, trends, patterns, data supported evidences, past incidents, and many more. It can give you the confidence to prove and support your past data findings and help reduce unwanted shocks and surprises that can give business stress due to missing future-proof data.

All data of an enterprise might not be relevant for that enterprise 10-20 or 50 years down the line. It is the responsibility of organizational stakeholders within an enterprise to coordinate with data architects to decide and earmark core entities and attributes relevant and useful for the business benefits even in the far future.

> *"Data Future Proofing" is a new phrase and is the process of anticipating the future and developing methods of capturing and arranging the data in a way that can minimize the gap due to missing data or relevant data for the purpose of relevance, data-driven researches, correlations, trends, patterns, data-supported evidences, past incidents, and experiences.*

We should not forget the importance of a data lakehouse for an enterprise. It is meant for the long term. Technology will keep evolving, employees, consultants, and vendors may come and go within an enterprise, but accumulated data relevance will always be there for an enterprise. Next-gen business is all about data. All cognitive activities (including cognitive science) revolve around the data you accumulate, whether healthcare-related or insurance. Aviation data, environmental, or weather data. Social, socio-economic data, or behavioral data. Geographical, political, or geopolitical data. Space data or the research data of any field of study. More past data or proven historical data can help in better future findings. Because, "Data is the New Gold."

> *Technology will keep evolving, organizations will keep changing, but accumulated data relevance will always be there for an enterprise.*

The most important question is, "Which data needs to be preserved, accumulated, stored, and saved for future purposes?" When creating a data warehouse or data lake, we think a few years ahead. It was never considered for decades or centuries. Here we consider the importance of data till eternity that can be passed from generation to generation. But we should be sensitive about its significance and relevance. We can't consider all gathered enterprise data as future-proof data. All data might not retain its relevance in the future. It will be a silly consideration and may lead to various problems, including but not limited to size, volume, policies breaches, and misinterpretations or misuses at later stages.

Future proof data should be capable of fulfilling any past data needs for various analytics and research purposes.

While considering future-proofing of data, we need to be sensitive about various aspects of data, including its relevance, relevant grain level, context, format, dimensions for different perspectives, future views, and viewpoints.

In this data context, a data view is what data you see and a data viewpoint is where you are looking from. Data viewpoints are a means to focus on the business data for particular aspects of the business. These aspects are determined by the concerns or business purposes with whom communication occurs to future-proof the data.

Remember, the data viewpoints may sometimes depend upon the stakeholder's perspective and may be subjective. Be a little generic while deciding the prospective candidates (which subjects, entities, attributes to be captured) for data future-proofing. A little generic does not mean 'taking everything' because being more generic may capture data that may not be useful in the future, and that will spoil the purpose of "Data Future Proofing."

Figure 9-4. Two different views of the same subject from two different viewpoints.

Data viewpoints are determined based on the business concerns and generally created in coordination with the core stakeholders.

Think about medical records. Capturing medical records is important. What is the value and benefits of historical medical records? What are all the benefits it brings to healthcare if utilized efficiently and effectively? Yes, it can help save human life. It can help in early diagnosis. It can help in medical research in many ways. It can help with faster vaccine creation for deadly health-related threats. It has the potential to reduce healthcare stress by many fold.

Take even the COVID pandemic scenario. If future-proofing would have been done for all the past medical records of similar epidemics or pandemics like Ebola, Avian Influenza, Mers, and H1N1, today's scenarios would have been far better.

But do you know how much privacy and confidentiality clauses a medical record carries? Handling medical records is a sensitive subject. Storing medical records at the application level has a different purpose than storing it in a data warehouse, data lake, or data lakehouse. When you bring a medical record to your data lakehouse, the purpose is not to treat a specific patient. Instead, the organization might utilize the medical records in the data lakehouse for various medical research purposes, early diagnosis, accurate treatment, preventive healthcare, and so forth.

Medical research, early diagnosis, proven treatment findings, or preventive healthcare methodology findings, do not require knowing the patient's name and Social Security Number. Do you really need the phone number of a patient diagnosed with the influenza virus in 1968 and was treated in a city hospital? You might need the age (or age group), sex, city/state, and certainly the medical conditions, including the symptoms, dates, diagnosis, treatment, and the result of that treatment.

Another very common scenario where data future-proofing can help from data vulnerability is an enterprise that captures personal and sensitive data. Personal data like name, address, medical details, and bank details and sensitive data like racial information, political opinion, religion, trade union association information, health, sex life, and criminal activity. The enterprise has been doing its business for more than two decades. All of a sudden, the company is acquired by another business house from a different domain or sector, such as a retail company acquired a software development company or a manufacturing company acquired a marketing research company. What will be the future of the personal and sensitive data captured by the first enterprise if data future-proofing was not done? There are chances of accidental exposure to those tons of personal and sensitive data kept by the previous organization. You never know if the new owning organization has the support to handle such data.

Data future-proofing can help reduce the data vulnerability risks for an enterprise.

Now let us discuss how data future-proofing is done.

We have divided data future-proofing processes into five different phases—Identification, Elimination, Future-proofing, Organization, and Storage.

Five phases of "Data Future-proofing"

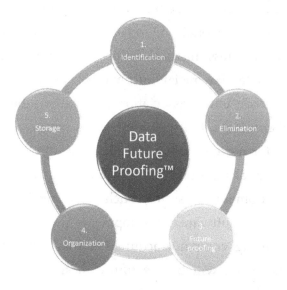

Figure 9-5. Five phases of data future-proofing.

Identification phase

Keeping the purpose of the future data in your mind (such as for analytics and research), identify all entities and attributes relevant and meaningful for various business needs and benefits. You need to identify only those future-proof entities and attributes of your business domain, such as healthcare, insurance, aviation, manufacturing, education, transportation, hospitality, and retail.

For example, the EMR might have hundreds of attributes in a healthcare domain, but you might need very few of them. The grain level of an EMR is up to every encounter of a patient. Still, for the future, you might need the extraction level from the disease, number of patients diagnosed with that disease, their gender, age group, cure status, and ultimate treatment.

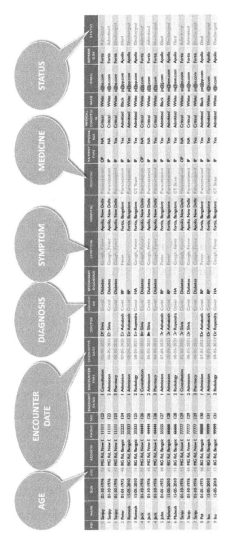

Figure 9-6. How to identify future-proof data and attributes.

> *The main purpose for future-proofing the data is to help execute analytics and research work.*

Elimination phase

Eliminate all those entities and attributes that have no significance for any future analysis or research. Eliminate sensitive, future sensitive, future proof, and controversial data. Follow an elimination method to be more specific—it helps narrow down data easily and quickly.

For example, how important is it to capture the shoe quantity a customer bought per order in the retail domain? Instead, we should focus on the type, color, or design of the shoes trending during every decade and what kind of shoes are trending today. This may give a perspective on fashion trends over time. This requires capturing information like shoe types, brands, periods, number of pairs sold, and so on.

> *Eliminate sensitive, future-sensitive, and controversial data while preparing your future-proof data sets.*

For example, on the facing page is EMR data from the healthcare domain. We had shown the future-proof data sets earlier. There are other types of data as well, like personal data, sensitive data, and controversial data.

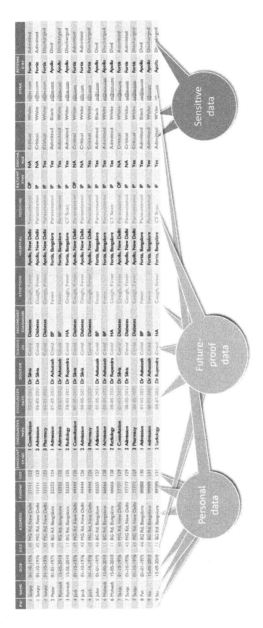

Figure 9-7. Personal, future proof, and sensitive data. Personal, future proof, and sensitive data are shown in blue and red color respectively.

You can understand that attributes are sensitive only if they are supported and served with personal data. For example, a patient's medical condition and diagnosis can be sensitive if supported and linked to personal information like Social Security Number. Similarly, the patient's race can only come under the controversial category of data if it is linked to the specific patient through an identifier or name.

In general, a data or data set contains its sensitivity or controversial nature only if it is linked or related to an individual's personal information. Else an isolated, abandoned, or unrelated sensitive or controversial attribute has no significance.

Future-proofing phase

By following phases 1 and 2, you have completed half of the future-proofing job. You identified only the data that will have relevance in the future. You eliminated all sensitive and controversial personal data. In addition, if you have data you think might not be fair to expose for future use, or that it might be misleading, or might bias any data analysis once exposed for future business purposes, you should anonymize it. Data to be concerned about is (a) personal data like name, address, medical details, and banking details and (b) sensitive data, like racial or ethnic origin, political opinions, religion, membership of a trade union, health, sex life, and criminal activity.

With data anonymization, you retain the purpose yet you don't expose the actual data.

These two categories of data might create biased decisions or may create controversies in the future. Especially category '(b)' is more sensitive for political subjects. Hence data anonymization will be a handy tool for this purpose.

Once you notice that a potentially sensitive or controversial attribute will be part of a future-proof data set, anonymize the associated personal information.

In most business scenarios, we do not need a detailed level or the lowest grain level of data for future use. The lowest level data is generally required in a transactional environment. Hence, we should judiciously decide the grain level of data while future-proofing your data. Deciding the required grain is a very important aspect while future-proofing the data. This will decide the volume of your future-proof data every year or decade.

The more data is aggregated, the less the chance of personal and sensitive data vulnerability.

Data in its lowest grain level are the raw form of records that may incorporate personal and sensitive data that are more vulnerable if not handled responsibly.

A data lake or data lakehouse can contain the lowest grain level of data. Hence, we need to be more sensible and preferably give priority to the data future-proofing features.

In principle, isolated, abandoned, or unrelatable sensitive or controversial attributes can be part of future-proof data because it has no significance until it is linked back to a person, place, or thing.

In a healthcare data use case, 50 years from now, one might not be interested in knowing whether 'Mr. Sanjay' (name) from 'New Delhi' (location/address) was a 'Hindu' (religion) and had COVID, and if he had, what was his CRT value? It might not solve any industrial problem, and it might not address any business issues at that time. Rather it might trigger some sensitive political issues or might fulfill biased interest. But suppose COVID or a similar type of virus resurfaces in 50 years. In that case, the healthcare industry might be interested in knowing the percentage of COVID-positive patients between 40-50 years of age and their average CRT value? What was the overall mortality rate? What were the recovery rates for the different age groups of people? Which medicine or drug showed the best results during its treatment? What were the infection spread ratios between males, females, and kids? What were the recovery rates in people with comorbidities?

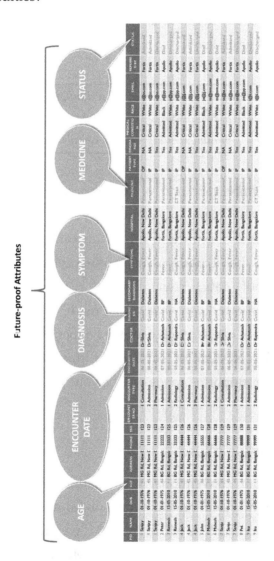

Figure 9-8. Future proof attributes in an EMR data set.

And such information requirements and fulfillment will address lots of business problems at that time. It may help healthcare professionals solve lots of healthcare issues. It may save many humans lives. So, it is evident that we may not have any reason to store data with the lowest grain level.

Future-proofing of data can help you eliminate unnecessary data burden, reduce storage, reduce data vulnerability and minimize enterprise data complexity.

The next important part of future-proofing is to future-proof the data capture cycle. Once you have decided the grain level and extraction level, you can write extraction rules, and then based on the capture cycle, capture your future-proof data. Your capture cycle can be daily, monthly, quarterly, or yearly. The mode of capture should be any supported storage mode, depending upon your destination system of storage. In this case, your data lakehouse supported mode will be your mode of storage.

Organization phase

Unlike your conventional organization of data into the destination system and like any special data management organization such as MDM or CDM, we propose having a separate **FDM**™ (Future-proof Data Management) layer in your destination data management, in this case, in the data lakehouse. If required, a separate data layer can also be proposed for the FDM. Please remember that FDM has nothing to do with MDM and CDM design or architecture. As MDM and CDM help manage enterprise data efficiently, FDM will help future-proof data be treated specially for future business benefits efficiently and strategically. So, this FDM layer should be treated special and designed by following all of these five phases of data future-proofing discussed in this section.

FDM is an implementation of an enterprise-wide system where the organization accesses its historical information for any future use from a single managed place. A central repository is created and all requests for future-proof data are satisfied from that one point.

The creation of an FDM system is not very complex. It is a repository of past business facts and figures. Keep the design simple and follow the five-phase process of data future-proofing.

FDM or future-proof data management allows the business to get their historical information at a single managed place for future purposes. A central future-proof data repository is created, and all requests related to future-proof data are satisfied from that one point.

Figure 9-9. The FDM (Future-proof Data Management) layer with a data lakehouse.

Storage phase

Once it comes to storage of FDM (Future-proof Data Management), an open format, generic platform-based system is recommended because data future-proofing is for the long term. Hence a proprietary or vendor-locked format or platform will not meet the overall purpose of data future-proofing.

> *Most of the Data lakehouse platforms support an open format of storage that is consistent with the basic requirements of the FDM.*

In this phase, you must ascertain the **accessibility** of the future-proof data sets. Who should have access to the data and have permissions to insert, update, and delete any data in FDM should be decided and ascertained in this phase only.

We must also determine the availability of the FDM. It is the nature of the FDM that it does not fall under 99.99999% availability requirement category. But yes, it should be available for any future use. The future can even be the next year of your business because this year's data is past data for you for next year.

Once you have ascertained accessibility and availability, storage upgradation is the last but not the least important strategy under this storage phase. Ensure the storage upgradation is done for the FDM where you have kept all your future-proof data to be accessed seamlessly using the latest storage platform year after year and decade after decade. Remember, data future-proofing is for eternity or until your business no longer exists.

Data lakehouse routine maintenance

The data lakehouse maintenance cycle is part of data lakehouse housekeeping.

Most data lakehouse platforms are self-maintained, and their framework has robust data governance and data management methodologies. But still, as the part of data lakehouse housekeeping, we should use these data lakehouse maintenance steps to keep the lakehouse in order year after year:

Figure 9-10. The data lakehouse routine maintenance lifecycle.

The secret of data lakehouse maintenance is in its successful implementation. We should automate most of the processes using the provided utilities or tools into a data lakehouse platform.

> *Meticulous planning and design of a data lakehouse supported with robust data lakehouse housekeeping, will lead to a great business benefit to the enterprise.*

CHAPTER 10

Visualization

What you see is on sale!

Visualization is a technology that helps you convert specific data into information using standard statistical, numerical, and graphical methodologies. That information is generally in a graphical or pictorial form and very easy for our brains to interpret and understand the value of the underlying data.

Raw data without appropriate visualization is like dumped construction raw materials at a building construction site. The finished house is the actual visuals created from those data like raw materials.

So, until you see the finished construction on that site, you only know that, yes, it is some dumped raw materials kept for construction. Until the construction is done, you did not know whether those raw materials were going to produce an independent house, villa, or apartment.

Similarly, in the context of an enterprise, you know that you have your ERP data, you have your CRM data, you have your financial transaction data, and tons of textual data in the form of enterprise business text that may include contracts, agreements, feedbacks, review comments, and logs. However, we are not sure how this data can be helpful for your overall enterprise business benefits. Specifically, your decision makers are not very conversant with raw data crunching like a data scientist or data engineer. In such cases, visualization comes to the rescue of data professionals to make that data presentable in various forms of dashboards, graphs, charts, and maps. It helps the enterprise in business decision-making as a vital decision support system. It can show the business trends. It can help draft the projection for the next quarter or financial year using the history of your business data.

For example, a hospitality company has many hotels and restaurant chains across the globe. As a best-case scenario, assume that they are now very organized and started using industry-standard applications and maintain state-of-the-art technology and infrastructure to run their show. Their ERP collects enterprise data across their chain of hotels and restaurants. Hotel booking data is collected using a cloud-based central booking system. Restaurant seat reservation data is done through a state-of-the-art mobile app. They have the industry's best CRM and loyalty applications to manage the customer profile, memberships, and loyalty points. They have every application they need to run the day-to-day business. All their applications are collecting tons of data every day. Data is getting piled up every minute.

But what next? Decision-makers of the business will not crunch the pile of data from different sources. They need technology to help them convert the data stored into their system to the information that can help them make better decisions. That technology can help make their strategic business plans for next quarter, next year, or even five years from now. A core business decision-maker or CxO might not be a data guy who can run the query, correlate various data entities, and get the information out of the raw data.

Turning data into information

Visualization techniques come in handy to data scientists, data engineers, and other data professionals working for that organization. With the help of visualization techniques and various statistical methodologies or cognitive science, the data scientist and data engineering professionals help the business decision-makers make strong and supported decisions to achieve short- and long-term business goals.

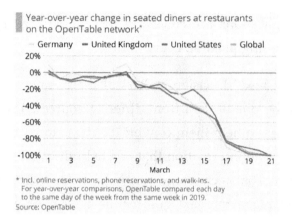

Figure 10-1. The impact (through year-over-year comparative analysis) of the lockdown on restaurant business due to COVID, during the first three weeks of March-2020.

Hence ultimately, the visualization can help the management understand the underlying business impacts on their bottom-line. For example:

- Year-over-year growth or loss
- Total sales and revenue
- Impact of a specific marketing campaign
- Overall revenue boosts due to increased customer retention rate using loyalty application in use
- Customer retention versus revenue boost correlation analysis

Another example can be from the healthcare domain. The healthcare industry has oceans of data including:

- Clinical data
- Pharmaceutical data

- Insurance data
- EMRs (Electronic Medical Records), including patient demographics and patient behavioral data
- Medical professional's master data records
- Imaging data
- Pathological findings
- Diagnosis

But do they use this data effectively? For example, they might have created a Health Information Exchange or Healthcare Data Hub. They might have a data lake or a data lakehouse. But what next? How are they using this data for healthcare betterment, including healthcare research? How can they achieve the true benefits of these gold mines of data?

The answer is, by converting data into information, they bring their business data to life. How can they bring their business data to life? By extracting all underlying meanings of associated industry or business data for the benefits of the healthcare industry. How can you convert your data to information? Visualization is one of the most effective ways.

The healthcare EMR data can tell healthcare professionals, including doctors, the data-supported reasons behind a specific disease. For example, how can a contagious disease spread? How can it be contained based on its behavior? Which medicine is showing better results against that specific disease? Which age group is most exposed?

If the answers to all these questions are available on time and at the fingertips of healthcare professionals, it will certainly be a great help to healthcare. It will help medical research find new upcoming viruses, strains, and mutations, and research medicines, vaccines, and life-saving drugs.

But this can only happen if we can present data as information in a consumable format. We need to know who is the consumer of the data. In this example, the consumers are medical professionals, pharmacists, biotechnologists, bioinformatics professionals, biochemists.

We need to identify the usable data, analyze the data, correlate it, and visualize it in a way that is easy to interpret by the end users.

What is data visualization and why is it important?

Data visualization is the graphical representation of data that helps visually show information hidden behind your raw data. Further, it helps translate data and information into a visual context. It is the illustration that tells a **story** behind the data.

We should not forget that the story component is key. Data visualization without a message is not information at all. It's just data.

Visualization makes data easier and natural for us to comprehend, understand and pull insights. Using visual elements like plots, charts, graphs, and maps, data visualization provides an accessible way to see and understand trends, outliers, and patterns in your large business data sets you store into your data lakehouse.

It is all about selecting what information to share, as well as how to share it.

These are the two fundamental choices in the creation of a visualization. Analysts do data visualization to deliver data in useful and appealing ways to users. Data visualization is about presenting large amounts of information in ways that are universally understandable or easy to interpret and spot patterns, trends, and correlations that directly help the end user extract all beneficial meaning out of their pile of data. Visuals and diagrams certainly make it easier for us to identify strongly-correlated parameters.

Difference between data visualization, data analysis, and data interpretation

Data analysis is the process of bringing order and structure to collected data. It turns data into information teams use for various purposes, including visualization. Analysis is done using systematic methods to look for trends, groupings, or other relationships between different types of data. As discussed earlier, data **visualization** is the process of putting data into a graphical representation like a chart, graph, or other visual format that helps inform analysis and interpretation for better comprehension and understanding by a human brain. Data visuals present the analyzed data in ways that are accessible to and engage different stakeholders. Multiple visuals will likely be needed to understand the larger change process and inform data use. Common data visual formats include:

- Frequency tables
- Cross-tabulation tables
- Bar charts
- Line graphs
- Pie charts
- Bubble charts
- Pictures
- Heat maps
- Scatter graphs
- Plots

Data interpretation is the process of attaching meaning to the data. Interpretation requires making conclusions about generalization, correlation, and causation, and answers key learning questions about your project. These three processes are not usually linear—they don't follow each other in an orderly process. Instead, they support, inform, and influence each other, resulting in super-rich and extremely useful data for any intended purpose or business.

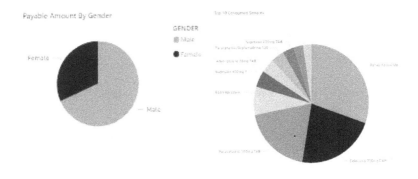

Pie   **Pie without legend**

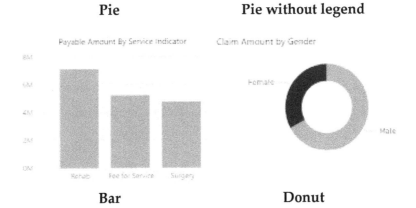

Bar   **Donut**

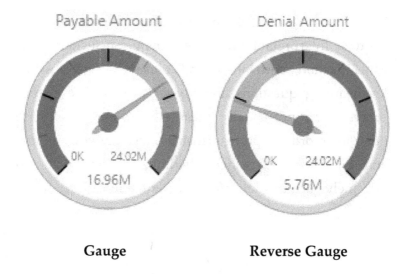

Gauge   **Reverse Gauge**

Figure 10-2. Commonly used visuals.

Figure 10-3 shows a few specially used visuals.

Correlation diagram
between two entities with
a root representation

Correlation graph extract
from a medical data set

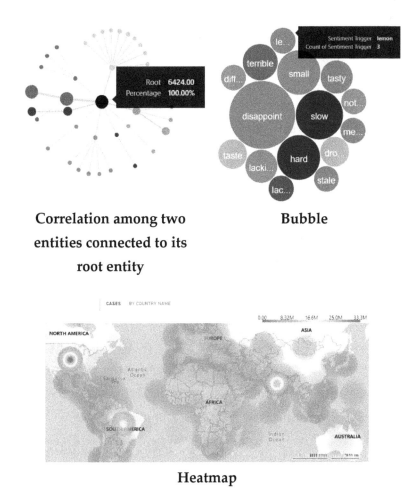

Correlation among two entities connected to its root entity

Bubble

Heatmap

Figure 10-3. A few specially used visuals.

Advantage of data visualization

The advantages of data visualization are many, and the common theme is that data visualization makes numbers accessible to everyone. For example, a CEO with minimal finance experience may not understand financial statements, but he will easily understand a negative bar chart! It's easier to display numbers with images. Though we should note here that data visualization is not limited to numbers—visualization can be done for text, context, and more. Numbers are the key behind visuals.

Another example is a sun next to the temperature to indicate warm weather or a dark cloud or water droplets to indicate rain. You might see a line chart to show GDP or population over time, or maybe a pie chart to show the number of men versus women who get COVID in Spain.

Moreover, imagine your state government wants to influence you by showing that their policies have helped improve the community. They want to show citizens that crime rates, death rates, and violence have all decreased since they have been in office. In this case, the best way to do so would be to show a line graph with a decrease over time for these variables.

As a list, here are some pros of data visualization that we'll explore further one-by-one:

- Ease of communication
- Attention earner
- Brings credibility
- Memorable or easy to remember
- Message enhancer

Ease of communication

Ease of communication means how easily, conveniently, or effortlessly you are communicating to the viewer what you want to show through your visual representation of data. There should be an obvious communicative value that comes from using data visualizations. It should be simply easier to understand rates and relationships when we express them visually. At the same time, we can use colors and simple labels to make the image even easier to understand. For example, this dashboard created on top of a lakehouse shows the Voice of Customers for a hospitality client (data and name scrambled for anonymity reasons).

Figure 10-4. The gauge indicator at the center of the dashboard shows that the negative sentiment of customers is on the borderline of the direct business impact (it is at the end of the green and about to enter the yellow zone). It is assumed here that up to 20% is a green zone and beyond that is a matter of concern for the business, and above 40% is dangerous for the hospitality or restaurant business.

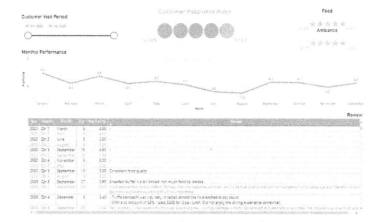

Figure 10-5. A visualization page shows the Happiness index for another chain of restaurants in a city.

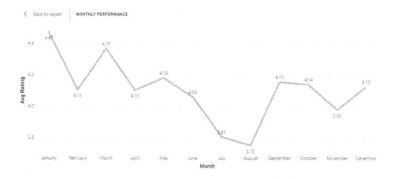

Figure 10-6. The overall monthly performance in terms of average ratings by the customers on various parameters of a hospitality business.

Figure 10-7. The Food rating by customers for a reputed restaurant of the city.

Figure 10-8. Even for a reputed restaurant, some factors bring in negative sentiments in their customers' feedback. Those who understood its importance on time and acted judiciously are doing well. Those who ignored its importance are doomed and out of business.

Attention earner

Your visuals should get the attention of the users. There's a good portion of the population that doesn't feel comfortable with numbers and numerical analysis. In fact, if you try to communicate relationships using any metric more complex than "rate" or "percent," you could lose a huge portion of your readers.

It's not because they're not intelligent. It might be because they just aren't interested in that kind of information—you simply don't *earn* their attention by doing so. But suppose you're able to display the relationship you want in a simple data visualization. In that case, you earn their thoughts and concentration, even for just a few moments or till they need to interpret, correlate, and consume.

Data visualization's key responsibilities and challenges include the obligation to earn your audience's attention—do not take it for granted.

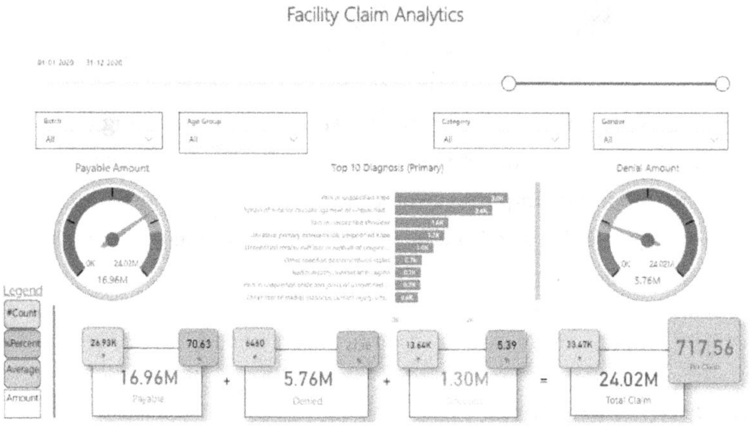

Figure 10-9. This screenshot of a dashboard-based visualization is from the health insurance domain. Facility, also known as hospital or healthcare provider, extends services to beneficiaries (patients). For services extended to patients, facilities must submit the incurred expenses as claims to the payers (insurance companies or the government). So, this dashboard shows the Facility Claim Analytics portion.

It gives the options of data filtration and shows that out of "Total Claim," how much is the "Payable" amount, how much was "Denied," and how much was the "Discount" on the overall claims? Depending on the agreement, discounts may vary from service to service or can be applied to the overall claim. Those two colorful dial gauges well placed within the dashboard work as "Attention Earner or Attention Grabber" and say whether the "Payable Amount" is judiciously and genuinely within the ideal range (in this case, about 80%). If the payable amount is below 80% of total claims, there are more denial and discounts than usual in the system. Hence, it may require re-checking to confirm that the payable is justified for that specific period (from 1st Jan 2020 to 31st Dec 2020). If it is below 60% of the total claim, then management needs to be on alert because more than 40% or rejection of claims or discounts is a concern and serious "attention earner." It clearly says that something is wrong in claims for that period. They need to investigate why so many claim rejections occurred?

At another hand, the right-hand side colorful dial gauge shows the "Denial Amount." The denial is within 20% range, so it might be justified (subject to the industry and conditions). But the moment the Denial/Rejection of claims crosses that 20% threshold, it becomes "Attention Earner," and that may need verification or cross-checks. But once the denial of claim crosses the 40% mark, it is a serious "Attention Earner." In such cases, management needs to investigate the claims of that period thoroughly. They should be convinced or satisfied with all the denial or rejection reasons. They should know that whether those denials were genuine or a blunder or mistake. If it is a mistake, they need to take corrective actions to fix it.

Brings credibility

Data visualization adds credibility to any message. It is well quoted in the past by various famous thinkers that the idea that a medium of communication changes the way the reader interprets it in the field of communication. Think about these three different media of communication:

- Text
- Television
- Digital radio or podcast

They focus on three different senses. A media can either be 'hot' or 'cold'. Hot media requires very little cognitive participation by its audience. However, cold media requires much cognitive participation by its audience. You can say that text is hot media, but a digital radio or a podcast is cold media. Text doesn't require the reader 'fill the gaps,' however, a digital radio or a podcast does.

Data visualizations are incredibly cold mediums because they require a lot of interpretation and participation from the audience. While boring numbers are authoritative, data visualization is inclusive.

Data visualizations absorb the viewer in the chart and communicate the author's credibility through active participation. Like a good teacher, they walk the reader through the thought process and convince him/her effortlessly.

Memorable

Visualization that is memorable or that leaves a long-lasting impression on your memory is more effective and complete.

Do you remember the exact word you read in a text last time? Do you recall an exact figure about an important topic? I don't remember either! However, I can easily still remember the dashboard we looked at earlier with a "denial amount" that was in the yellow zone and a denial of claim with more than a 20% threshold.

Figure 10-10. Perhaps the most important advantage of data visualizations is how easy they are to remember.

Message enhancer

The right data visualization works wonders to enhance the message you want your audience to get across. More than just memorable, the right graph communicates how you want data to be communicated to your audience. For example, two people looking at raw data see two different stories, and they build graphs to communicate their message.

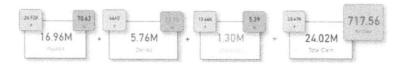

Figure 10-11. The denied amount is 5.76 million.

Figure 10-12. This dial gauge shows the same message.

We can clearly see that the dial gauge visual is more powerful and convincing to management or the end user. The following figure, therefore, works as a "message enhancer."

However, both visuals show the same thing, same number, and same figure. But one is just a boring number, and another is an alarm or attention grabber used here as a "message enhancer."

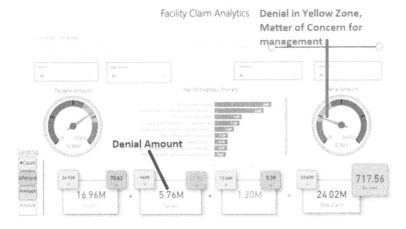

Figure 10-13. Both figures were part of the same dashboard, but one simply shows the boring numbers to complete the calculation for number buffs (users who love to play with the numbers). And another for the management that needs to be alerted for anything wrong with that number!

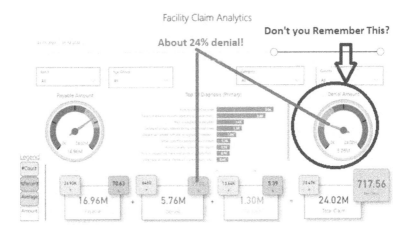

Figure 10-14. Message enhancer.

Importance of filters in visualization

Filters give you the freedom to pan across and the opportunity to visualize more. It reduces the unnecessary clutter in your visualization, helps maintain the hygiene and purpose of the visualization, and gives more flexibility to select, verify, correlate, and cross-verify.

Figure 10-15. A few filter options frequently used in visualizations. Filters can be time, entity, or attributes of the subject to be visualized.

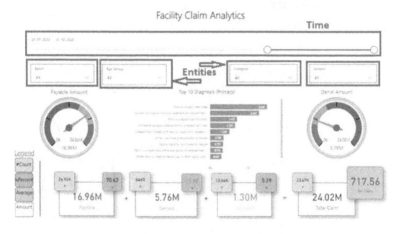

Figure 10-16. The filter can help utilize the same visualization in multiple ways by applying different filters on the same visualization.

Various data lakehouse architectures-based frameworks available in the market provide open APIs for direct access to files with SQL, R, Python, and other languages.

For example, Databricks supports various types of visualizations out of the box using the display and displayHTML functions. Databricks also natively supports visualization libraries in Python and R and lets you install and use third-party libraries.

Once you have your data lakehouse, visualization is possible by languages too. Python, R, Scala, and SQL are very good companions for visualizing data directly from your data lakehouse.

CHAPTER 11

Data Lineage in the Data Lakehouse Architecture

O ne day a financial analyst is asked to go out and create a report for management. Management asks, "What has been our corporate revenue for July?"

The analyst searches a database and finds that corporate revenue for July was $2,908,472.00. Management looks at the report and becomes irate. Management says that can't be the right number. The credibility of the work the financial analyst has done comes into question. In a state of desperation, the analyst sets out to determine the accuracy of the number reported to management. The analyst finds the number in a database full of other KPIs.

```
Corporate monthly revenue
July: $2,908,472
```

The analyst then asks the question—how was this number in the KPI database calculated? In fact, what does this number mean? The number can mean booked revenue, projected revenue, or actual cash revenue, depending on who is asked. The analyst is surprised to discover that these numbers are three very different things.

Just looking at the final value that has been calculated tells you almost nothing. To be useful, you have to know exactly what has been calculated, what data was used in the calculation, and how the calculation was done. When the analyst starts to investigate, the analyst finds out that the calculation of the number results from a circuitous path of previously made calculations and data movements.

The chain of calculations

The start of the chain of calculations is a payment made in Matamoros, Mexico, and is in Mexican pesos. Before the payment can be entered into the organization's books, it must be converted from pesos t dollars.

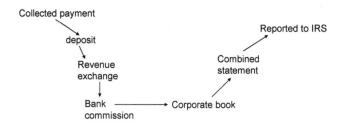

Figure 11-1. Then there is a banker's commission on the handling of the payment that must be calculated. Then there is a transfer fee. Only after all these things are done does the payment enter the corporate books. By this time, the collected payment value is very different from the received money into the corporate account.

The circuitous route that has been described is but one of many paths that information goes through. Inside the organization, the information flows from one system to the next. By the time any piece of data reaches a database, the data may have gone through many selections and transformations.

The circuitous flow that has been described is true in one way or another for almost every type of data—not just revenue. For example, consider the flow of demographic data through a geographical system. Data is collected in Dallas, Texas. From Dallas, the information flows into a county collection agency. Next, the information flows from the county collection into a regional collection, then into a state collection, a national collection, and a North American collection.

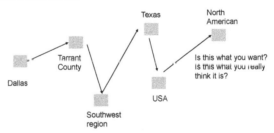

Figure 11-2. At every level, the data passes through a selection and calculation process. When the data arrives at the highest level, there is no telling what the data represents. Different cities may use different algorithms along the way. Houston may calculate things differently from Dallas. And Austin may have their own selection and calculation. By the time the data reaches a high level, all sorts of data may be mixed together based on all sorts of calculations.

Selection of data

And the passing of data from one station to the next is not the only issue with the integrity of the data. There is also the issue of the selection of data. For example, it is one thing to say that you have corporate payments. But are there some types of corporate payments that have been missed? Does Dallas have the same selection criteria for payments as Houston? As El Paso? As Austin?

It is normal for there to be different selection processes throughout a large infrastructure.

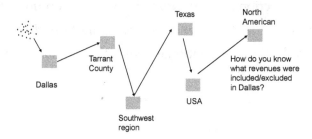

Figure 11-3. If there are different selection criteria in different places, how can the summarized number be accurate? Or even understood?

Algorithmic differences

And the selection criteria for data is not the only issue. Every time data passes through an algorithm, there is the chance that the data is calculated differently, from one algorithm to the next.

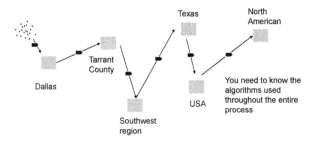

Figure 11-4. To have iron clad consistency of the data, every algorithm the data passes through must be known and synchronized.

The process of passing data through many systems illustrates what happens to data inside the organization. For the analyst to have confidence in his/her information, the analyst needs to have the information along with its lineage. In the case of structured information, the kinds of lineage that are required are:

- The step of processing that is being described
- The name of the data being considered
- The algorithm identification that the data has passed through
- The date the algorithm was executed
- The selection criteria for the data passing into the algorithm

The lineage information required is needed for each step that the data passes through. It is not sufficient to merely document one or two steps. Instead, we need the lineage documentation for all steps.

Lineage for the textual environment

Lineage information is needed throughout the data lakehouse. Lineage information is needed not just for structured information, but also for textual data. The good news is that lineage information for textual data is much easier to locate and manage than lineage information in a structured environment. The reason lineage information is easier to handle in the textual environment is that lineage information is regularly captured by textual ETL.

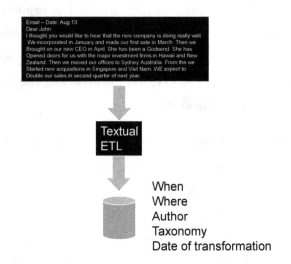

Figure 11-5. When text is passed through textual ETL.

One of the byproducts of passing raw text through textual ETL is capturing and storing the metadata that is part of the document. This makes it natural and easy for organizations to capture and store lineage information from text.

Lineage for the other unstructured environment

The third type of data in the data lakehouse is other unstructured data. The data lineage for other unstructured data is just as necessary as for the other environments, but nevertheless quite different.

It is normal for much of the data created for the other unstructured environment to be created by machine. This is because machine measurements are made continuously. At the start of collecting other unstructured information, an identification of the machine making the run and the date of the run is typically captured.

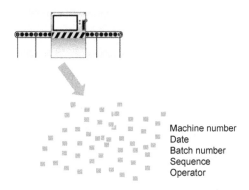

Figure 11-6. Each of the measurements is captured in a database that ultimately finds its way into the data lakehouse. The measurements of lineage all relate to this origin of other unstructured data.

The other unstructured data lineage information typically consists of:

- Machine number—the specific machine making or monitoring the part or equipment being made
- The date the part or equipment was made or monitored
- The batch number the part is associated with
- The sequence of the part in the batch being monitored
- The name of the operator of the equipment

Of course, the specifics of the lineage information in the other unstructured environment will vary from one type of equipment to another. The specifics for lineage information for other unstructured information shown here are only suggestions.

Data lineage

However it is done, the specification and the disclosure of the data lineage is an important piece of information for the data lakehouse.

structured	textual	other unstructured
Step number	When	Machine number
Data name	Where	Date
Algorithm id	Author	Batch number
Date executed	Taxonomy	Sequence
Selection criteria	Date of transformation	Operator
Number of records		

Figure 11-7. Data lineage is absolutely necessary for the analyst to understand how to do analysis properly.

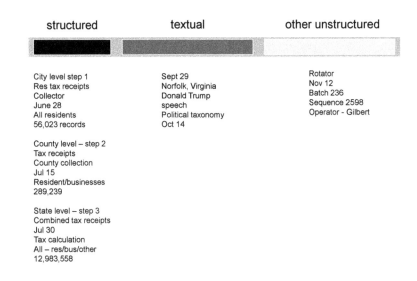

Figure 11-8. An example of how some actual lineage information might look.

CHAPTER 12

Probability of Access in the Data Lakehouse Architecture

Consider the query that has to search through a lot of data to find a single record. Of course, we can build an index to avoid having to do a sequential search. But what if the query is run only on an infrequent basis. If the query is done infrequently, building an index to service the request makes no sense. Or what if the structure of the data does not support indexing? Worse case, the search through the database must be done sequentially, from one unit of data to the next.

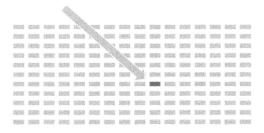

Figure 12-1. Finding the needle in the haystack.

There are several challenges to finding the needle in the haystack. The first challenge is that of complexity. The logic to find the record supplied by the end user and the programmer to find the record may be fierce. And however it is done, the system's work required to execute a large, sequential search is enormous. If an index is built, there is the overhead of the maintenance and the creation of the index. If there is no index, there is the overhead of having to search many records sequentially. We should avoid large sequential searches for needles in the haystack.

Efficient arrangement of data

It is much more efficient and much simpler to arrange to have the data that is needed to be located in a closely contiguous, easy-to-find manner.

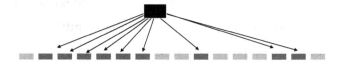

Figure 12-2. Efficient and simple access of data.

In this case, the data is organized so that the needed records are near each other. As such, the records are easy to search and efficient to find.

It may be farfetched that such a change in architectural approaches is difficult to achieve—either an efficient way to organize data or an inefficient method. But in actuality, it is easy to achieve this arrangement of data.

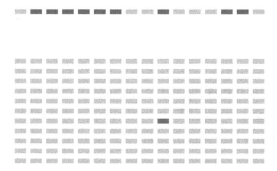

Figure 12-3. Two very different ways to organize the same data.

Probability of access

The way to physically arrange the data is in accordance with its probability of access. When you look at any large body of data, you find that some data is frequently accessed and other data is infrequently accessed. This phenomenon occurs with all bodies of data.

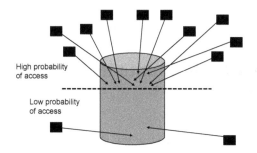

High probability of access

Low probability of access

Figure 12-4. Some data is popular to access and process, and other data is not so popular. The data that is not popular is often called "dormant data."

The criterion for discerning where the dividing line between the two types of data is different for every organization. However, some common criteria for determining where data is or is not accessed are:

- **How old is the data?** Current data is almost always accessed more frequently than older, dormant data.
- **What types of data are accessed more frequently?** An experienced engineer can tell you how to use data to troubleshoot a manufacturing process. The experienced engineer knows what types of data to look for and what types of data to ignore.

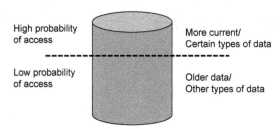

Figure 12-5. Criteria used to discern the dividing line between the different types of data.

Different types of data in the data lakehouse

The need to discern between different types of data is different in the data lakehouse environment. The data lakehouse contains three essentially different types of data:

structured, textual, and other unstructured data. The sheer volume of these different types of data is very different. There is little structured data in the lakehouse. There is more textual data in the lakehouse than structured data. And there is a lot of other unstructured data in the lakehouse, more than that found in the structured or textual environment.

The process of dividing data along the lines of differences in terms of access probability is called the "segmentation of data."

Relative data volume differences

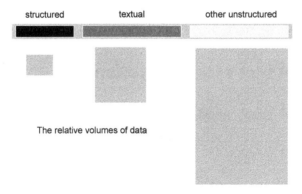

Figure 12-6. The relative differences in the volumes of data found in each environment.

Because of the different volumes of data found in the lakehouse, the segmentation of data based on probability of access must be applied to other unstructured data. It is less important that the technique of segmentation be applied to textual data. And it may or may not be necessary to apply the technique of segmentation to the structured data.

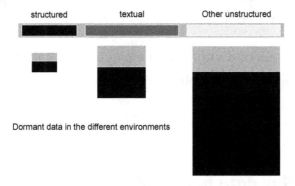

Figure 12-7. The differences between active data and dormant data in the data lakehouse environment.

Advantages of segmentation

There are many good reasons for segmenting data in the data lakehouse based on the probability of access. But the two most important reasons are:

1. By segmenting data, the data is simpler to process

2. By segmenting data, there can be a considerable saving in storage costs and processing costs

Using bulk storage

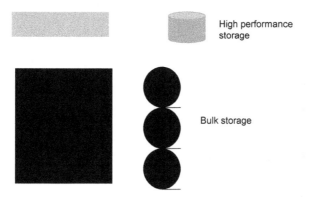

High performance
storage

Bulk storage

Figure 12-8. By dividing the data along the lines of highly used data
and dormant data, the designer can take advantage of significant
differences in storage costs. Expensive high-performance storage
can be used for popular data, whereas less expensive storage can
be used for dormant data.

It is simply true that dormant data will be slower and
more cumbersome to access and analyze. But given the
fact that it is rarely analyzed, this limitation is not much of
a burden.

Incidental indexes

However, if there is a need to expedite processing in the
dormant data environment, the designer can always create
one or more incidental indexes. An incidental index is an

index that is not created for a specific need but is created for expediting potential needs that may arise in the future.

And certainly, more than one incidental index can be created for dormant data.

Since many records are found in the dormant data environment, creating an incidental index is a slow and tedious process. That's the bad news. The good news is that these indexes are created in the background, where there is no rush to create the index.

Incidental indexes

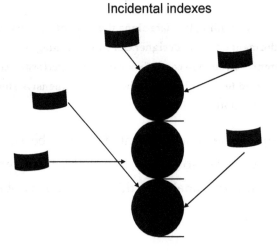

Figure 12-9. When it comes time to analyze dormant data, the incidental index is there waiting to be used.

CHAPTER 13

Crossing the Chasm

The essence of the data lakehouse is the mixture of different kinds of data. Each type of data has its own distinct properties and serves different communities with different business purposes.

It is true that the different kinds of data can be placed in the data lakehouse and can be used to serve only their individual constituents. But there may be even greater value when the data in the lakehouse serves multiple communities at the same time.

Merging data

It is necessary to merge the data for more than one community of users to be served by more than one type of data. In the simplest of cases, a simple join is required. In more complex cases, creativity is required.

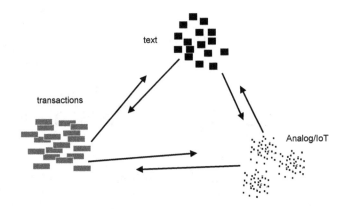

Figure 13-1. The problem is that the data in the data lakehouse is widely variant in form and content.

Different kinds of data

The first and most immediate challenge in merging the different kinds of data found in the data lakehouse is that the data format in the different environments varies quite a lot. For example, text is placed into a standard database format compatible with structured, transaction-based data using textual ETL. In that regard, mixing the format of structured data and textual data is quite simple. But the key structure of transaction-based data may or may not be compatible with the key structure of textual data. In some cases, there is compatibility. In other cases, there is no compatibility whatsoever.

The analog/IoT data format is usually very different from either textual data or transaction-based structured data.

And the key structure of analog/IoT data is normally very different from transaction-based or textual-based data.

A real challenge is merely getting through the different types of data formats and finding common ground on which to base analysis.

Different business needs

But an even greater challenge of using combined lakehouse data lies in combining the different types of data to meet a business need. It is like taking an Inuit Eskimo from Alaska, a tribesman from New Guinea, and a camel herder from Egypt, and mixing them together. There simply is very little cultural similarity between the three types of people. As a result, communication and cooperation become a challenge.

Crossing the chasm

To make full use of the data found in the data lakehouse, it is necessary to cross the chasm of technology and business functionality that separates the different environments.

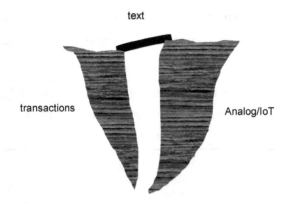

Figure 13-2. There is a chasm between the different kinds of data.

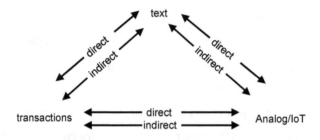

Figure 13-3. There are two distinct ways to cross the chasm. There is the direct approach and the indirect approach.

Each of the different types of data has their own unique characteristics. In the direct approach, data is simply moved from one environment to the next. Then, a match is made on a key and the data is linked together (if, in fact, a match can be made at all). To make sense of the resulting merged data, there needs to be a common key structure between the different environments. If there is no common key between the two environments, it is almost impossible for the data to be meaningfully merged and analyzed.

When there is a common key among the different environments, the common key that is likely to exist can take many forms—product, name, Social Security Number, address, state, time, and so on.

The blending of the data found in the data lake that is done indirectly is much more powerful and useful than the direct blending of data. And there are many forms that the indirect blending of data can take.

Consider a simple example to understand how different data types from the data lakehouse can be indirectly blended together.

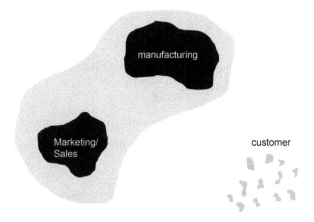

Figure 13-4. Suppose there were three entities: a body of customers, a company with a marketing and sales organization, and a company's manufacturing arm.

The customer makes their voice heard in many ways. Email is one channel that the customer uses. Another channel is the Internet. Yet another is the call centers that most organizations have. In each of these channels, the customer expresses his/her opinion. And the customer has opinions about everything. For example, the customer has opinions about the cost of things, how to install things, power outages, the weather, the quality of a product or service, the color of a product, and so on. And in a small or a large way, each of these opinions is valuable to the company.

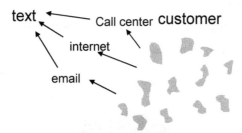

Figure 13-5. However they are expressed, these customer opinions are captured in the form of text.

The manufacturing arm of the organization generates its own data. One of the places where that data is generated is in producing the product made by the organization. The machines used to produce the product generate measurements of all sorts of things. The speed of manufacture, the quality of manufacturing, the content of the goods being manufactured, the flow of progress to the final product—are all measured.

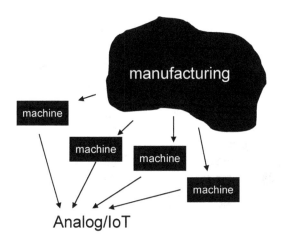

Figure 13-6. These measurements are gathered into an analog/IoT
database.

The third place that data is generated is in the marketing
and sales arm of the organization. One of the places where
data is generated is in the transaction created by making a
sale. The date of the sale, who the customer is, the sales
price, the salesperson, and the sale location are just some
of the information created by the sales activity.

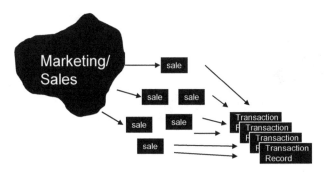

Figure 13-7. These sales information units of data are directed to a
database.

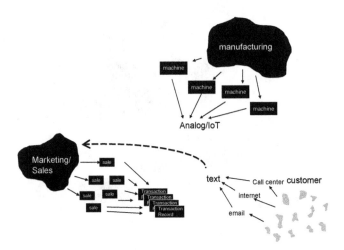

Figure 13-8. The voice of the customer is heard, and the results are fed to marketing and sales. Marketing and sales then make adjustments to the products produced and adjustments as to how the products are marketed. The result of the adjustments that marketing and sales make ultimately show up in new sales transactions.

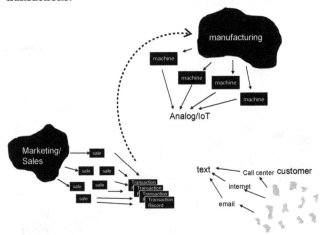

Figure 13-9. The sales transactions are measured and the results are fed to manufacturing. Manufacturing then adjusts schedules, objectives, and the roadmap based on actual sales.

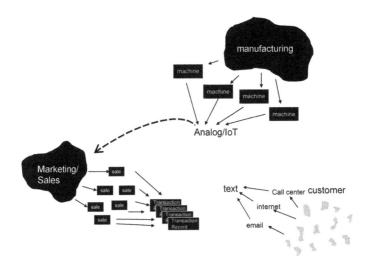

Figure 13-10. The manufacturing data is fed to the marketing and sales department. The kind of data that is fed includes shipment dates, order completion dates, advisories of delays, information about quality, and so forth. Marketing and sales use this information in sales forecasts, delivery scheduling, contracts, and so forth.

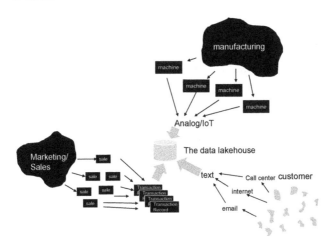

Figure 13-11. As the data is collected from different sources, it is loaded in the data lakehouse.

The scenario depicted here reflects many organizations but certainly not all organizations. However, there is an indirect marketing loop for other types of organizations that is similar to the one described.

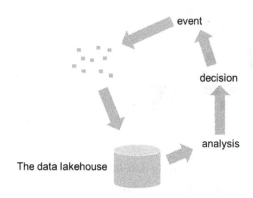

Figure 13-12. The indirect feedback loop that the data participates in looks like this.

Data—in whatever form it is in—is taken from the lakehouse. Analysis is done leading to a decision. A decision is made, and the decision leads to some sort of event. The event generates data which is then fed back into the data lakehouse. This then is the indirect path taken by the data found in the data lakehouse. Thus, the chasm of data found in the data lakehouse has been crossed in a very indirect fashion.

CHAPTER 14

Managing Volumes of Data in the Data Lakehouse

There are many challenges to the economic and technical management of the data lakehouse. One of the largest challenges is managing the sheer volume of data collected in the data lakehouse. There are lots of reasons why there are large volumes of data that are aimed at the data lakehouse:

- Data needs to be collected over time—there may be five years, ten years, and even more data in the data lakehouse
- Data needs to be collected at a low level of granularity in the data lakehouse—the low level of granularity implies that there will be lots of units of data that are collected
- Data is generated from a wide variety of sources, including text, analog, and IoT—the sources of data are almost endless

There is then an avalanche of data headed for the data lakehouse.

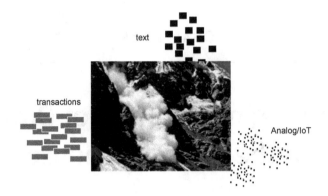

Figure 14-1. An avalanche of data.

Distribution of the volumes of data

The volumes of data found in the data lakehouse are not normally distributed evenly. Usually, the least amount of data is structured, transaction-based data. Then there is textual data. Then having the most amount of data in the data lakehouse is the analog/IoT environment.

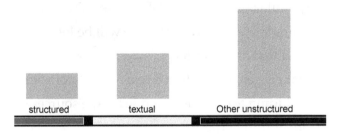

Figure 14-2. The volumes of data found in the data lakehouse are not normally distributed evenly.

And throughout all the levels, the phenomenon of dormant data being found in a large volume of data is always present. Whether there is structured data, textual data, or analog data, there is always dormant data found in any large collection of data.

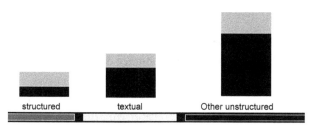

Dormant data in the different environments

Figure 14-3. How much dormant data is there, where is it located, and how fast is it growing?

High performance/bulk storage of data

Because there is dormant data in the data lakehouse, it is convenient that there are different types of storage media for data. There is high-performance storage data and there is bulk storage of data.

Data needs to be distributed over the different types of storage based on the probability of data access. The high probability of access data needs to be placed in high-performance storage, and the low probability of access data needs to be placed in bulk storage.

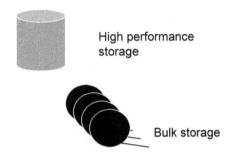

Figure 14-4. High-performance storage allows data to be accessed quickly but is expensive. Bulk storage does not allow data to be accessed quickly, but bulk storage data is inexpensive.

This storage arrangement is good for the efficient access of data and for the economics of storing data. When data is placed as described, it is said to be "segmented."

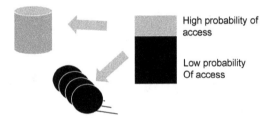

Figure 14-5. From a strategic standpoint, segmenting data is the best practice that to manage large volumes of data.

Incidental indexes and summarization

However, other practices can be employed to manage large volumes of data. One of those practices is the creation of "incidental" indexes. Incidental indexes are created by background processes that are run against the bulk data when not in use. Incidental indexes are for the low probability access data.

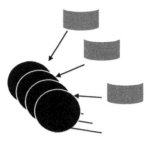

Figure 14-6. Creating one or more incidental indexes can save enormous amounts of time if the need to access bulk data ever arises. And given that one or more incidental indexes are created in background processing, it is inexpensive and not inconvenient to do the processing necessary to build the incidental indexes.

Another technique to manage large volumes of data is the judicious use of summarizations or aggregations. Used strategically, summarizations can minimize the need for searching large amounts of data. In many cases, it makes sense to place summary data in high-performance storage and to place the underlying detail in low probability storage.

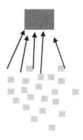

Figure 14-7. Summarization is often a good idea.

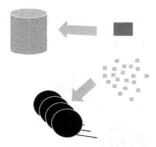

Figure 14-8. The summarized data is placed in high-performance
storage.

Periodic filtering

Another approach to the management of large amounts of
data is to employ periodic filtering of data. Monthly,
quarterly, or annually the data is filtered from high-
performance storage to lower performance storage based
on the age of the data. As data ages, it is less in demand.

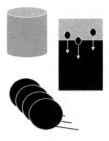

Figure 14-9. Periodic filtering of data is useful.

Although filtering can be done based on data other than
date, date is the most common criteria for filtering data.

Tokenization of data

Another more Draconian approach to the management of large volumes of data is that of tokenization of data. In tokenization, data values are replaced by shorter values. For example, the word "Pennsylvania" can be replaced by "PA." While tokenization can reduce the volume of data significantly, tokenization introduces problems on data access and analysis. To analyze the data, the tokenized data must be converted back to its original state, which in many ways defeats the whole purpose of tokenization. For this reason, tokenization is an extreme measure:

```
Pennsylvania—PA
Babe Ruth—BR
James Dean—JD
Argentina—AR
Wednesday—WD
Arlington Cemetery—AC
November—NO
```

Separating text and databases

In the same vein, when it comes to textual data, one strategy to reduce the volume of data needed is to place the contextualized data in high-performance storage and place the underlying text in bulk storage. Again, this arrangement works nicely as long as there is no great need to cross the boundaries of storage types frequently.

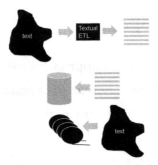

Figure 14-10. Raw text is placed in bulk storage; the database is placed in high-performance storage.

Archival storage

And finally, there is archival storage, which can store data as it moves out of bulk storage. As a rule, archival storage is less expensive than bulk storage but is much more awkward in the usage of the storage. Therefore, if there is any reasonable probability of access, data should not be placed in archival storage.

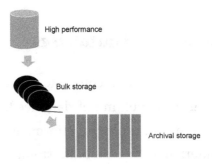

Figure 14-11. A third level of storage further alleviates the issues of massive volumes of data.

Monitoring activity

Yet another approach to managing very large volumes of data is monitoring the activity going against the data. By monitoring the activity going against the data, the analyst has a very precise idea of what data should be placed in bulk storage and what data should be placed elsewhere.

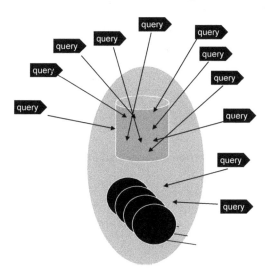

Figure 14-12. Monitoring activity against the data lakehouse.

Parallel processing

Another approach to managing large volumes of data is that of parallelizing the processing that needs to occur. The notion behind parallelizing the processing of data is that if one processor takes an hour to process data, then two processors will take half an hour to process the same data. And parallel processing indeed reduces the amount of time required to process a workload.

But there is a limitation to parallel processing, and that limitation is that parallel processing only reduces the total length of time that is required to process data. Thus, parallel processing actually raises the cost of processing significantly. Nevertheless, parallelizing a workflow can reduce the time required to process data.

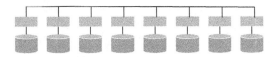

Figure 14-13. Parallelization reduces total processing time but increases expense.

CHAPTER 15

The Databricks Lakehouse Platform

In the previous chapters, we covered the concepts and benefits of a data lakehouse architecture, such as transaction support, schema enforcement, BI support, openness, and the requirements for diverse workloads with structured and unstructured data types, as well as support for end-to-end streaming.

Here we dive deeper into one specific implementation of a data lakehouse: the Databricks Lakehouse Platform and its workloads.[2]

Overview

As you may know, Databricks has been the pioneer and champion in the field of data lakehouses. Founded by the creators of Apache Spark, MLFlow, and Delta Lake,

---

[2] Chapter written by Databricks.

Databricks has developed a cloud-based platform that combines a data lake's scalability and economics with a data warehouse's functionality and performance.

Figure 15-1. Data lakehouse architecture.

In this chapter, we will explore the features, capabilities, and implementation of the Databricks Lakehouse Platform in more detail.

We will discuss how the Databricks Lakehouse Platform enables users to easily and efficiently process and analyze large amounts of batch and streaming data, and how it integrates with other tools and technologies in the data ecosystem.

So, if you are interested in learning more about the implementation of the data lakehouse concept, the Databricks Lakehouse Platform that serves more than seven thousand customers, and how it can help your organization harness the value of its data, keep reading!

Lakehouse: A new generation of open platforms

Databricks is the inventor and pioneer of the data lakehouse architecture. The data lakehouse architecture was coined in the research paper, *Lakehouse: A New Generation of Open Platforms that Unify Data Warehousing and Advanced Analytics*, introduced by Databricks' founders, UC Berkeley, and Stanford University at the 11th Conference on Innovative Data Systems Research (CIDR) in 2021.

At Databricks, we continuously innovate on the lakehouse architecture to help customers deliver on their data, analytics, and AI aspirations. The ideal data, analytics, and AI platform needs to operate differently. Rather than copying and transforming data in multiple systems, you need one platform that accommodates all data types.

Ideally, the platform must be open so you are not locked into walled gardens. You would also have one security and governance model. It would not only manage all data types but also be cloud-agnostic to govern data wherever it is stored.

Last, it would support all major data, analytics, and AI workloads, so that your teams can easily collaborate and get access to all the data they need to innovate.

What is the Databricks Lakehouse Platform?

The Databricks Lakehouse Platform unifies your data warehousing and AI uses cases on a single platform. It combines the best elements of data lakes and data warehouses to deliver the reliability, strong governance, and performance of data warehouses with the openness, flexibility, and machine learning support of data lakes.

This unified approach simplifies your modern data stack by eliminating the data silos that traditionally separate and complicate data engineering, analytics, BI, data science, and machine learning. It's built on open source and open standards to maximize flexibility. And, its common approach to data management, security, and governance helps you operate more efficiently and innovate faster.

The Databricks Lakehouse Platform architecture

Data reliability and performance for the lakehouse

Delta Lake is an open-format storage layer built for the lakehouse that integrates with all major analytics tools and works with the widest variety of formats to store and process data.

Photon is the next-generation query engine built for the lakehouse that leverages a state-of-the-art vectorized engine for fast querying and provides the best performance for all workloads in the lakehouse.

Unified governance and security for lakehouse

The Databricks Lakehouse Platform provides unified governance with enterprise scale, security and compliance. The Databricks Unity Catalog (UC) provides governance for your data and AI assets in the lakehouse—files, tables, dashboards, and machine learning models—giving you much better control, management, and security across clouds. Delta Sharing is an open protocol that allows companies to securely share data across the organization in real-time, independent of the platform on which the data resides.

Instant compute and serverless

Serverless compute is a fully managed service where Databricks provisions and manages the compute layer on behalf of the customer in the Databricks cloud account instead of the customer account.

Customers benefit from serverless because:

- it brings a truly elastic, always-on environment that's instantly available and scales with your needs.

- it eliminates management overheads for clusters: Serverless eliminates the burden of capacity management, patching, upgrading, and performance optimization of the cluster.

- it lowers infrastructure cost: Under the covers, the serverless compute platform uses machine learning algorithms to scale compute resources right when you need them. This enables substantial cost savings without the need to shut down clusters manually.

Databricks Lakehouse Platform workloads

The Databricks Lakehouse Platform architecture supports different workloads such as data warehousing, data engineering, data streaming, data science, and machine learning on one simple, open and multicloud data platform.

Data warehousing

Data warehousing has been one of the most business-critical workloads for data teams since the 1980s. Today the best data warehouse is a lakehouse for the following reasons:

- The Databricks Lakehouse Platform lets you run all your SQL and BI applications at scale with up to 12x better price/ performance, a unified governance model, open formats and APIs, and your tools of choice — without any lock-in.

- **Databricks Photon** is a next-generation query engine designed that provides the performance for data processing. It is a key component of the Databricks SQL platform, which is built on top of the lakehouse architecture.

- Reduce resource management overhead with serverless compute, and easily ingest, transform and query all your data in-place to deliver real-time business insights faster.

- A **SQL warehouse** is a serverless compute resource that provides instant, elastic SQL compute decoupled from storage, and will automatically scale to provide unlimited concurrency without disruption for high concurrency use cases.

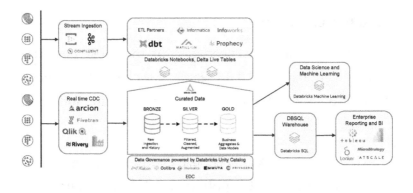

Figure 15-2. Modern Data Warehousing on Databricks.

Data engineering

Data engineering on the Databricks Lakehouse Platform allows data teams to unify batch and streaming operations on a simplified architecture, streamline data pipeline development for ELT/ELT and testing, build reliable data, analytics and AI workflows on any cloud platform, and meet regulatory requirements to maintain governance.

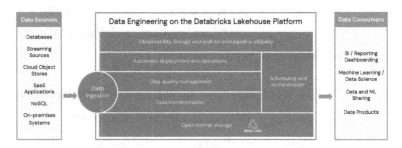

Figure 15-3. Data engineering in the lakehouse.

The Databricks Lakehouse Platform supports a data engineer in ingesting, transforming, and orchestrating data.

Simplified data ingestion

Ingest data into your Databricks Lakehouse Platform and power your analytics, AI, and streaming applications from one place. There are two easy, popular options for ingesting data into the Databricks Lakehouse Platform:

- Auto Loader incrementally and automatically processes files landing in cloud storage in scheduled or continuous jobs without the need to manage state information. It efficiently tracks new files (scaling to billions) without having to list them in a directory and can also automatically infer the schema from the source data and evolve it as it changes over time.

- The COPY INTO command makes it easy for analysts to perform batch file ingestion into Delta Lake via SQL.

Automated ETL processing

Once ingested, raw data needs to be transformed for analytics and AI. Databricks provides powerful ETL capabilities for data engineers, data scientists, and analysts with Delta Live Tables (DLT). DLT is the first framework that uses a simple declarative approach to build ETL and ML pipelines on batch or streaming data, while automating operational complexities such as infrastructure management, task orchestration, error handling and recovery, and performance optimization.

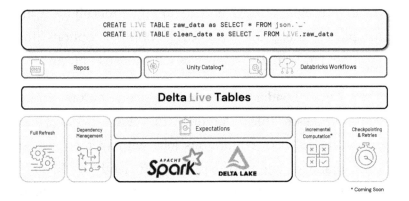

Figure 15-4. Data lakehouse ETL.

Since DLT pipelines are plain SQL or Python code, engineers can easily apply software engineering best practices like testing and monitoring, and also use their CI/CD toolset to deploy reliable pipelines at scale.

Reliable workflow orchestration

Databricks Workflows is the fully managed orchestration service for all your data, analytics, and AI that is native to your Lakehouse Platform. Workflows orchestrate any workload on any cloud, including Delta Live Tables and Jobs for SQL, Spark, notebooks, dbt projects, ML models, and more. Deep integration with the underlying Lakehouse Platform ensures you will create and run reliable production workloads on any cloud while providing deep and centralized monitoring with simplicity for end users.

Figure 15-5. Data lakehouse orchestration.

Data streaming

Data streaming is one of the fastest-growing workloads within the Databricks Lakehouse Platform and the future of all data processing. Real-time processing provides the freshest possible data to an organization's analytics and machine learning models enabling them to make better, faster decisions, more accurate predictions, offer improved customer experiences, and more. The Databricks Lakehouse Platform dramatically simplifies data streaming to deliver real-time analytics, machine learning, and applications on one platform.

Streaming data ingestion and transformation begins with continuously and incrementally collecting raw data from streaming sources through Auto Loader or directly ingesting from message brokers such as Apache Kafka or Amazon Kinesis. Once the data is ingested, it's transformed from raw into clean data with a schema appropriate for downstream analytics, ML, or applications. Delta Live Tables (DLT) makes it easy to build and manage these data pipelines at scale. DLT is a high-level abstraction built on Spark Structured Streaming, a scalable and fault-tolerant stream processing engine.

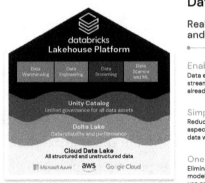

Data streaming made simple

Real-time analytics, machine learning and applications on one platform

Enable all your data teams
Data engineers, data scientists, and analysts can easily build streaming data pipelines with the languages and tools they already know.

Simplify development and operations
Reduce complexity by automating many of the production aspects associated with building and maintaining real-time data workflows.

One platform for streaming and batch data
Eliminate data silos, centralize security and governance models, and provide complete support for all your real-time use cases.

Figure 15-6. Databricks Lakehouse Platform.

Real-time analytics refers to the downstream analytical application of streaming data. With fresher data streaming into SQL analytics or BI reporting, more actionable insights can be achieved, resulting in better business outcomes.

Real-time ML involves deploying ML models in a streaming mode. This deployment is supported with structured streaming for continuous inference from a live data stream. Real-time modeling has many benefits, including shorter latencies for predictive maintenance or credit card fraud detection.

Real-time applications process data directly from streaming pipelines and trigger programmatic actions, such as displaying a relevant ad, updating the price on a pricing page, stopping a fraudulent transaction, etc. There typically is no human-in-the-loop for such applications.

Data science and machine learning

Data science and machine learning (DSML) on the lakehouse is a powerful workload that provides a data-native and collaborative solution for the full ML lifecycle. It can maximize data and ML team productivity, streamline collaboration, empower ML teams to prepare, process and manage data in a self-service manner, and standardize the ML lifecycle from experimentation to production.

The main features of the Databricks DSML platform are as follows:

- **Exploratory data analysis**: The platform allows users to explore and visualize data easily and supports various languages such as R, SQL, Python, and Scala. It has built-in visualizations and dashboards, and allows for code sharing and collaboration with features such as co-authoring, commenting, automatic versioning, and Git integrations.

- **Model creation and management**: The platform offers tools for data ingestion, model training and tuning, and production model serving and versioning. The Databricks ML runtimes are optimized and preconfigured with popular libraries such as scikit-learn and XGBoost, and support distributed training and hardware acceleration with GPUs. From within the runtimes, you can track model training sessions, package, and reuse models easily with MLflow, an open source machine learning platform created by Databricks. MLflow is included as a managed service within the Databricks Lakehouse Platform.

- **Feature Store:** Databricks ML has a built-in feature store for creating and exploring features, selecting them for training and scoring machine learning models, and publishing them for real-time inference.
  No Code: If you are looking to get a head start,

AutoML allows for low to no-code experimentation by pointing to your data set and automatically training models and tuning hyperparameters to save both novice and advanced users precious time in the machine learning process.

- **Model versioning, monitoring, and serving:** Once the models perform well, they must become part of a pipeline that keeps models updated, monitored and available for use by others.

Databricks can help here by providing a world-class experience for **model versioning, monitoring, and serving** within the same platform that you can use to generate the models themselves.

The modern data stack

The Databricks Lakehouse Platform is open and provides the flexibility to continue using existing infrastructure, to easily share data and build your modern data stack with unrestricted access to the ecosystem of open source data projects and the broad Databricks partner network with Databricks Partner Connect.

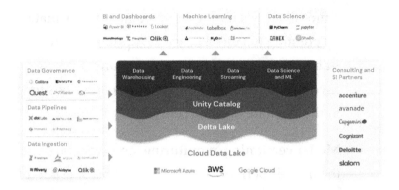

Figure 15-7. Databricks thrives within your modern data stack.

Databricks Technology Partners integrate their solutions with Databricks to provide complementary capabilities for ETL, data ingestion, business intelligence, machine learning, and governance. These integrations allow customers to leverage the Databricks Lakehouse Platform's reliability and scalability to innovate faster while deriving valuable data insights.

Global adoption of the Databricks Lakehouse Platform

Today, Databricks has over 7,000 customers, from Fortune 500 to unicorns across industries doing transformational work. Organizations around the globe are driving change and delivering a new generation of data, analytics, and AI applications. We believe that the promise of data and AI can finally be fulfilled with one platform for data analytics, data science, and machine learning with the Databricks Lakehouse Platform. Now data and AI can be harnessed and used to advance strategic business outcomes.

Learn more

- Lakehouse: A New Generation of Open Platforms That Unify Data Warehousing and Advanced Analytics
- Databricks Lakehouse Platform
- Databricks Lakehouse Platform Demo Hub
- Databricks Lakehouse Platform Customer Stories
- Databricks Lakehouse Platform Documentation
- Databricks Lakehouse Platform Training and Certification
- Databricks Lakehouse Platform Resources

Index